RISE OF THE WARRIORS

By Mark Esch

Foreword by Matt Birk

Rise of the Warriors

ISBN: 978-1-6755753-1-4

DEDICATION

This book is dedicated to God.

To my wife Sarah, we are the best team in the world.

To my three beautiful daughters, my life would not be complete without you.

To my parents Linda and Rick and my older brother Darryl. Thank you for your love and support through the years.

To everyone, and there are so many, who have touched my life throughout the years. Thank you.

Titus 2 6-8

CONTENTS

Rise of the Warriors

Rise of the Warriors

Rise of the Warriors

ACKNOWLEDGMENTS

There are so many people to thank when undertaking a journey like this. First and foremost, I'm thankful for my relationship with Jesus Christ. I'd like to thank the community of Caledonia for your support. My hometown of Brownsville, Minnesota. I'd like to thank all the former players and coaches who contributed whether by interview or just being a part of this tremendous program. I'd like to thank Carl Fruechte, Ernie Hodges and Mark Froehling. These men have always been there for me. All the people who I've been able to do life with the last 42 years, thank you.

Thank you to Ryan Pitts, Vision Media, LLC., for the photos and book cover.

A special thanks to my family, to my wife and editor, Sarah Esch. You are the best.

Foreword

Everything changed when I showed up for the first day of football practice in my sophomore year of high school. I had been a very average athlete up to that point in my life. I loved sports but wasn't very good at any of them. I had tried all of them, except football, so I figured I didn't have much to lose. That summer and fall, I discovered God gave me a very specific talent— I had the knack for getting in peoples' way and grabbing onto them. These skills are very useful for an offensive lineman. That day I became a football player.

For the next 22 years, I didn't just play football— *I was a football player*. It wasn't just an annual autumn kind of thing, it was 365 days a year. If it was in-season, my focus was on whoever we were playing that week. In the off-season, it was about lifting weights, drinking protein shakes and reading bodybuilding and strength magazines trying to find the "secret" workout to getting bigger and stronger. Upon waking every day, a lot of my mental energy was focused on how and what I was going to do that day to become a better football player.

Now that might sound unhealthy, but let me explain why I don't necessarily agree. You see, in football, talent is irrelevant. First, I don't know of a high school football team that makes cuts. In other words, if you show up every day and aren't totally averse to contact, you can be on the team. And not just be on the team, but contribute in meaningful ways. Football has 11 players on offense, 11 on defense, 11 on each and every special team. Because there are such a variety of positions on the field, you need guys that are big and small, fast and slow, graceful, and brutish. There is a spot for anyone and everyone— all you have to do is pay the price of admission.

Second, because football is the ultimate team game and physicality is such a big part of it, talent means about zero once the ball is kicked off. Ninety-five percent of football is preparation. Everyone needs to be on the same page on each and every play about their assignments; otherwise, you have no chance. And if a team doesn't show up in the right state of mind, they will get beat. Winning football games is never easy. It's going to hurt a little bit. There is no way around it.

So when someone says they are a football player, I think it speaks to their character. Showing up every day, putting in the work, delaying gratification, sacrificing for the good of the team— these things go beyond football. These are things that make you successful in life. Football is more than a sport. It's a classroom where lessons and virtue aren't just taught, they are learned. The game is only the vehicle for forming people.

If you have played the game or been around it, none of this is news to you. If you're not familiar with football, you might be surprised by the "good in football" because today much of the conversation around the game is negative— concussions, dropping participation levels, NFL players behaving badly, etc. Yes, there are risks associated with playing football, but intelligent conversation needs to be balanced. You have to talk about the rewards that come with playing football as well. Almost half of the boys in our country don't have a father in the home. For many of these boys, that void is being filled by their high school football coach. For others, a football team is the family they long for- where they are loved and accepted unconditionally. Teaching young people that if you want to be successful, you need to be disciplined and think about others before yourself. Millions of former high school players view the experience as being transformational.

Rise of the Warriors is a story that needs to be told- we need more beauty, goodness, and truth in our world today. Carl Fruechte is as fine of man as you will meet. His job title is high school football coach, but his purpose is to help boys become men and reach their full potential as people, husbands, fathers, and leaders. He does that as well as anyone. Winning state championships is a by-product of that because football always has been and always will be about people. A football team is a family. When someone feels the love of a family, they can do things they thought were beyond them.

I used to play football, but I will always be a football player.

Matt Birk- former NFL player and Super Bowl champion

PREFACE

I've told my wife for years that I needed to write a book about Caledonia football. A 1995 graduate of Caledonia High School, I was amazed at the change in culture that occurred over the years. Someone needed to tell the story, even write a book. I may have mentioned the book idea one too many times to my wife because she told me, "You just need to stop talking about it and do it." With Sarah's support and encouragement, I set out on an endeavor to communicate what has taken place in this small Minnesota town.

The intent of this book is not to boast about a 68 game winning streak. It's not to tell you about 10 state titles in fourteen years. Undoubtedly, there will be readers who are drawn to this story because of the winning streak and the state championships. However, the purpose of this book is to show how a football program's culture can change a team, a school, and a community— for generations to come. I want to paint a picture that football is a safe game that can make a positive difference in the lives of our young people. Teenagers need an outlet. It can come in many forms, but I believe football to be the best way a young man can learn teamwork, commitment, discipline, and the people skills necessary to thrive in life. Because of the physical nature of the game, it's an outlet especially needed in the teen years. Many young people also fall in love with training for football and transfer that into a life filled with exercise and fitness.

In this book, you will hear stories from people that were instrumental in the development of the outstanding culture of brotherhood and service that has been established in Caledonia. Many people have contributed throughout the years, and those people are or were essential to the process. But one name will appear more than any other in this book. That name is Carl Fruechte. No matter who I talked to as I gathered information for this book, everything came back to Carl. In the end, Carl Fruechte is Caledonia football. And his story deserves to be told. He's not perfect and will be the first to admit that. At times in this book, it may sound like he is the Superman of football coaches. This is not true; he is human. But he is a great football coach, and all of us can learn lessons from him in both life and football.

I want the world to see that football is a safe game. No one that has played for Caledonia in the last twenty years or longer suffers from CTE or life maiming injuries. Maybe that stuff is more prevalent if kids choose to play college football or move onto the NFL. High school football is still an extremely safe sport. In fact, the high school level has benefited the most from the safety advances in the game. Do kids still get hurt? Do serious injuries still occur at times? Yes. But most who have played the game at the high school level would not trade their experience for anything. In many cases, including mine, the game of football has helped them stay focused on high school academics.

Student-athletes who have gone through the Caledonia football program do, however, benefit from learning life skills that make a difference. The culture was toxic before some key role models showed up, such as Mark Froehling, Ernie Hodges, Brent Schroeder, and Carl Fruechte. Many would say Caledonia was suffering from toxic masculinity. The transition from "toxic" masculinity to a culture of humility, selflessness, and sacrifice is the real story here. From a toxic culture to a culture of good character. That's the purpose. That's the story.

On a personal level, the great game of football has literally saved my life on several occasions. The game has been doing the same for many in Caledonia and across the country for years. When used correctly, high school football can be a tool to teach young men life skills and change the trajectory of their lives. At a time in our history when many would like to see full contact sports eliminated from our public schools, I believe that football has never been more critical to our educational system. I believe the mental health of teens and pre-teens is declining, in part, due to instant access of information at their fingertips, both positive and negative. Football is a way to reach our young people and teach them the skills necessary to navigate their ever-changing world. Why is football so effective? It's a tough sport. It's a challenge. Young men take on this challenge and become better people because of it, especially when it's done the right way.

So how did football save my life? In my junior year of high school, I experienced a bout of depression. I have never shared this until now, but I struggled with life and purpose. Thoughts of suicide entered my mind. Fortunately, I never came close to acting on those thoughts, but I was certainly down and out for a while. I have no doubt God put football in my life to give me something to look forward to because, during that time of depression, I looked to my senior year of football with hope and excitement. As you will learn in this book, it did not disappoint. Though we didn't win a championship, it gave me hope. It gave me something to belong to that was bigger than myself.

In the years following my senior season, the depression lifted, but I got caught up in the alcohol and party scene in college. Looking back, I'm not proud of my behavior, but as all tough times do, it led me down a path that made me the person I am today. The underlying theme through all of this for me was Caledonia football. I was at many of the games we will talk about in this book. At one point early in his head coaching tenure, Carl even threw me in the press box and was asking my advice. I wasn't even on the staff! Many times I was right there on the sideline. In addition to the support of my family, Caledonia football became my safe haven. A place where I could get away. It gave me something to get me through life.

I started to develop my own football life during this time. A good football player but never great, I tried out for the University of Wisconsin-La Crosse football team. At the time, La Crosse was a powerhouse NCAA Divison III program. In 1996, I was cut after the spring tryouts. The following year I was cut after the fall two-a-days. With the support of Carl and Caledonia strength coach Ernie Hodges, I never quit and made the team as a running back in 1998. Both Ernie and Carl were in attendance at a key scrimmage in my tryout that year. Along with my family, they have always been there to support me. Being a senior, I decided to end my football playing career after 1999 two-a-days. It was a tough decision, but I needed to graduate from college and move on.

During this time, I had fallen in love with strength and speed training and cut my forty yard dash time from 4.8 to 4.5 seconds through hard work and determination. I was able to come back to Caledonia and work out in the weight room in the summers while hanging around Carl and Ernie. In fact, I still attended Ernie's Sunday night squat sessions and worked out with many of the people you will read about in this book. I was also blessed to start giving back to Caledonia football by sharing the new Olympic lifting techniques I was introduced to while at UW-La Crosse. I remember being excited to go back to Caledonia and show Carl and Ernie what I had learned. It's interesting to reflect on the days where I was able to help out the players, including Carl's son Isaac, who I taught to power clean when he was about eight years old. I didn't know it at the time, but Isaac would spend two seasons in the NFL. To me, he was just an annoying, stubborn little kid. He has now become a great man.

When my college career ended, it allowed me to attend more Caledonia football games, and I was able to watch the program evolve. Being a health and physical education major and passionate about football, I knew I would be a coach someday. I dreamed of being a head football coach at the Division I level. I enjoyed spending time in Caledonia watching games. I enjoyed talking with Carl and Ernie. Carl drove to La Crosse many times to hang out and talk about life and football. He was a great friend and resource for me as I began to build my life as a coach.

My career took another step in the right direction when I was walking to class in Mitchell Hall at UW-La Crosse. My former coach, Roger Harring, had just retired. I bumped into him in the hallway. He stopped me and said, "Hey Esch, you should try to hook on as a student assistant with whoever they hire to take the program over." I said, "Thanks, I think that's a great idea." I took Coach's advice to heart. When Larry Terry, the former offensive coordinator, was promoted to the head coaching position, I volunteered to work a summer football camp. Coach Terry came by and saw me running drills and teaching skills. After practice was over, he said, "Mark, you need to make coaching your career. We should try to get you a graduate assistant job at a college football program." I was excited and committed to being a student assistant with the offensive line and junior varsity offensive coordinator at UW-La Crosse as I finished my degree. This was an excellent experience for a first-year coach!

This led to an exciting coaching career with stops at a great program ran by the late Bob Jackson at White Bear Lake High School in Minnesota. I was promoted to the varsity staff after working at the youth camp that summer. My next step was a graduate assistantship at the University of South Dakota, it was full of frustration and struggle, but in retrospect a great learning experience. The experience was so negative I left after one year unsure if staying in football was the right decision. However, my coaching career was resurrected by Tim Hermann, the head football coach at Austin High School in Minnesota. I went from a negative experience to a fun and highly enjoyable experience with Coach Hermann. After three seasons as the offensive line coach in Austin, I received my first head coaching offer. As a 29-year-old with no head coaching experience, Mankato West High School took a chance on me as their coach. What followed was an amazing eleven season stretch that ranks 9th in the history of Minnesota football winning percentage. Through the hard work of so many committed players, coaches, and community members, we had a record of 106-23 and two state championships.

My experience growing up in Brownsville, Minnesota, and attending

Caledonia High School was a tough one, but it made me who I am today. I've had many close friends through the years, but my relationship with Carl Fruechte, Ernie Hodges, and Mark Froehling has been consistent in my life. Watching what Mark Froehling started as the head coach in the early '90s and what Carl took to a new level in the late '90s to the present day has been a fantastic experience. This program is evidence that football makes a difference, not only in the lives of coaches and players but when done right, football has a significant impact on school culture and community culture. This program has produced countless winners in life, young men who will continue to contribute to making the world a better place. The most notable are the two United States Navy SEALs and a pair of NFL football players the program has produced. But just as important are the former players who are making a difference in other professions or life in general, as husbands and fathers. The lessons they take away from being part of Caledonia football are invaluable.

Most importantly, I am thankful to God. In 2004 I put my trust and faith in Jesus Christ. This has been the most impactful decision I have ever made or will ever make. I didn't need football to save my life any longer. Jesus Christ saved my soul 2000 years ago. I had a sense of belonging through my faith that I cannot explain. Most of the behaviors I struggled with melted away. Do I still have struggles? Absolutely. Am I perfect? Far from it! But my faith has centered my life and given me a purpose in all things, including football. As a head coach, I wanted to win every game I coached, but I never attached value to winning. I attached value to the process and the relationships that make this game great. God has given us all things as tools to be used to benefit others. Football is now a tool that I use to make an impact.

I came to understand later in life that Carl and Mark were also men of faith. Centering their lives on Christ has meant everything to them. When a person applies principles of true Christianity to their life, everything improves. For Carl and Mark, their faith is a guiding beacon, a lighthouse that grounds them and refines them in every area of life.

We don't achieve perfection, but we move in the right direction when we put our faith in Christ.

I will be forever grateful I was born in the small town of Brownsville, Minnesota. I had a family that loved me but allowed me to make mistakes and learn on my own. Every day, I was bussed to school in Caledonia. Yes, personally, I experienced many pains and struggles along the way, but it built who I am. God has used each and every experience to make me a better person, no matter how miserable life was at the time.

The story that follows about Caledonia football is more than a story; it's a legacy. I add in my own experiences along the way. My viewpoints may not be shared by everyone who went through the school at the time I did, but the stories are absolutely true. There are critical themes in these stories that apply not only to football but to all areas of life. At a point in our country where we struggle to find leadership, we can look to this small town in Minnesota and learn what it takes to create positive change. The same principles can be used to change a business, a state, a country, or even the world.

CHAPTER 1

November 16, 2014, was a cold, wintry Saturday afternoon. The snow had piled up across a large part of Minnesota. I was nine years into my tenure as head football coach at Mankato West High School. Our team had loaded up the bus, and we were on our way to the state semifinals. We had a matchup with a tough St. Michael-Albertville team led by up-and-coming football coach Jared Essler. Typically, these games were played indoors. The warm confines of the Metrodome were a place the weather did not matter. With the dome gone and U.S. Bank Stadium being constructed in its place, all of our games, including the championship game, would be outdoors. Our team was in pursuit of a second state championship under my tenure. We were a balanced spread offense with the potential to score a lot of points with fast, explosive athletes.

Our bus churned through the freshly plowed highway en route to Eden Prairie High School. The game time was 6 p.m. My concern, as we took the 75-minute bus ride, was all about the weather. I know, I shouldn't have worried about events beyond my control. But as a coach, worry is a problematic vice to master. I certainly could not control the weather by worrying, but that did not seem to matter. We did our best to prep the kids for the playing conditions. We had made a point to talk to the team about the snow and cold, and how best to handle it mentally and physically. The Tuesday pre-practice talk concluded with one of our linemen raising his hand to say, "Coach, what you are saying is, don't be a wimp." Yes! That's exactly what I was saying. It was great to hear a senior player make that comment, it provided the right mindset for the week. The laugh he got from the team actually helped us loosen up, and the practices were excellent leading up to the game. Our team's attitude left me with no concerns about our mental capacity to handle the elements. Still, my worry continued. We had a great defense, so I knew we would always have a chance to win. But how would this weather affect our scheme? Our pass game? Our ball handling and footing? This was my concern.

However, my mind had another concern. I was tracking my former high school as they played on the very field we were soon to arrive at. Eden Prairie was hosting several games that day, back to back. The score kept updating in the opponent's favor. My alma-mater, Caledonia High School, ultimately lost the game. I had followed Caledonia Warrior football since my days as a high school player. I even showed up at practices and games when I had the time. I coached track with Carl Fruechte, their head coach, and I always felt a connection to the school where I grew up. I regularly talked with two former coaches, Mark Froehling and Carl. Mark was the head coach when I played. He had moved on from Caledonia in the late 1990s and took a job in Farmington, Minnesota. Mark eventually worked his way up to being the head coach and had some outstanding teams. He was a tough, hard-nosed, power football coach. Mark was the type of guy who always cared about you beyond the field. I was happy that he was my football coach in high school. We had some great experiences.

Carl was similar but different in some ways. Carl is consistently more vocal, a bit more intense. I think Carl hates losing more than anyone I know. So, I was a little nervous to call him after the loss, which had literally just become final. I wanted to ask him about the field conditions to help ease my mind. I dialed up his number and listened as the phone rang. It was 2014, and he carried around a phone that looked like the first one I owned in 2001. Carl answered the call a little down-and-out and rightfully so. "Hey, Carl. Tough one, eh?" I said when he answered. Carl replied in a depressed but respectful manner, "Yeah, Mark. They (the BOLD Warriors) had a good team. They outplayed us today. Their kids made more plays than our kids. They deserved to win." Carl always pays respect to his opponent in a loss, and a victory, for that matter. "How were the field conditions?" I asked. "Not good," Carl replied. "The footing was tough for the kids. The field is snow-covered. Conditions were not great." We talked for another minute or so. I thanked him, and he wished us luck. He genuinely wanted us to win and was willing to help out however he could.

That conversation five years ago may seem insignificant, but I will always remember it. It was the last time Caledonia High School lost a football game.

A School of Dominance

Why has Caledonia Football been so dominant over the last decade and beyond? What makes a team so successful in the win-loss column? It is a complicated question to answer. Ten state championships within fourteen years— 68 wins in a row. Why is it almost impossible for most to duplicate? People are searching for answers that could help lead them on a similar path to success. Whether you are looking for success in athletics or any area of life, a story like the one that is unfolding in this small Minnesota town is intriguing. How does a city of around 2,800 become so consistently dominant? They are similar to every other small town in Minnesota. They can't recruit players. They don't get open enrollments or transfers. What is the underlying factor to their massive success on the field?

Here's the thing, the art of success is readily available to everyone. Many times, it's right in front of them. So many people become clouded by the world and the distractions around them that they don't see it. Things just get in the way. Some people get caught up in the non-essentials, and they don't even realize they are missing critical aspects that lead to success. As we study Caledonia Football, we will see it is different. It's different in a way that is attainable to everyone willing to put in the work, apply the discipline, and check the negative pride and ego at the door. But most are not willing to pay the physical, mental, and emotional price that comes with high-level success. Most people will tell you that great teams just "get all the talent." These teams are "so lucky, they have all the skill." "It's easy for them because they have the best athletes." "They have it on cruise control." People who believe these things are doomed immediately. They will never achieve consistent success because they are breaking a rule. That rule? No excuses. No matter how tempting or easy those excuses are.

You may have thought you were doing everything right with your team the last five, ten, or fifteen years. But you are probably wrong. Some points you are missing altogether; others might just require some fine-tuning. The people who will achieve success at a consistent level are those who will be totally honest with themselves, find their weaknesses, and work tirelessly to fix any holes in their philosophy. It took Caledonia over a decade of relentless determination to reach peak performance. It is a process of minimizing weaknesses and maximizing strengths.

Noteworthy success is not achieved through passivity. But, people confuse themselves. They think they are defeating passivity with hard work. Hard work is essential, yes. However, a critical analysis of leadership philosophy, mental approaches to work, relationships, interpersonal skills, and many other subtle, yet vital pieces must be put together to achieve greatness. These are the types of work that seem to get ignored. In short, leaders need to work as hard on themselves as they do on their X's and O's or their business plan. By working to improve themselves, they will begin to see the directly proportional relationship of character— both team and individual— to consistent success. Follow through, accountability, role-modeling, clear and direct communication, and relationships are just a few of the attributes that must be continuously improved upon to reach peak performance.

It goes beyond the "success" on the football field. Plenty of programs win consistently, but few produce champions both on and off the field. Why is that? You will learn that Caledonia emphasizes not only football skills but life skills. It's a constant battle. No one will completely master the craft, but what started with Mark Froehling in the '90s, Carl Fruechte has nearly perfected.

The kids that have gone through the Caledonia football program are not flawless. That's impossible, and it's not the picture I am trying to paint. The program, kids, parents, and community as a whole have had struggles. The coaching staff continually battles mental demons that try to attack every human being. "Am I doing enough?" "Am I staying humble through the process?" "Could I be doing more?" The difference in Caledonia football, when doubts arrive and when fear strikes, players and coaches fight back. Throughout the years, the teams and coaches have managed chaos, uncertainty, and fear. The Caledonia Warriors go on the offensive when these liars show their ugly heads.

After graduation, some kids from Caledonia High School (which also includes the small towns of Eitzen, Freeburg, and Brownsville) choose to stay local to build a life in a small town that offers a slower pace and a stable community. Many will find physical work, blue-collar, if you will, in construction, home repair services, some small business ownership, etc. These are all highly respectable jobs, and the people who stay in this area are hard-working, honest, and trusting. Like almost all midwestern small towns, these people are the backbone of America. These families are also the cornerstone of Caledonia football. They stay in the area to raise families and support the school system and community. Some young people choose to leave the small-town life to venture out and give city life a try. The people who leave Caledonia have also experienced success.

Caledonia football does coaching the right way, and it spills over into personal life. The real success of the program is starting to emerge and will continue to be recognized for the next several decades as these former players continue to invest in their communities and the world. Just ask former player and Carl Fruechte's son-in-law Troy Frank, "It's like the kids that go through the program come out with an advantage in life. It is hard to explain, but employers want Caledonia football kids to work for them. The people of Caledonia know how to work hard and commit. So much of this is a credit to the football program and the culture it has helped create in the Caledonia school system and beyond," Frank said.

It is simply unbelievable, but Caledonia and the group of small towns that feed into the high school total a population of 3,500. In the last decade or so, these small towns have produced two NFL players, two Navy SEALs, state champion caliber high school coaches, talented strength and speed coaches, and many other former students who have been successful in life on a variety of levels. The program is also producing less visible success. Leaders at home and in the community who are every bit as successful in their endeavors.

It's essential to understand the intangibles that must be studied, practiced, taught, and modeled to reach a person's true, full potential. It is also important to understand success. Yes, winning sixty-eight games in a row and several state championships are a success. But more importantly, we need to understand the definition of success as coined by John Wooden: "Success is peace of mind, which is a direct result of self-satisfaction in knowing you made the effort to do your best to become the best that you are capable of becoming." Success in life is not just winning championships, becoming a Navy SEAL, or NFL football player. No, if this were the criteria for success, we would be inundated by failures in this country. In fact, about 99 percent of the population would be deemed failures.

This leads us to the fact that everyone in life can be a success. You may not be rich and famous, but achieving the peace of mind that John Wooden talks about is more valuable than money or fame. A rich person without peace of mind is a failure. The highly motivated person that achieves financial success, but in the process allows his family to fall apart, is failing. The John Wooden philosophy is what Caledonia has captured and put on the football field. Everyone has the potential to get better. Everyone has the potential to maximize their God-given talents by hard work. It's also important to understanding their strengths and weaknesses while working diligently to be the best person they can be. Eliminate hate, envy, and self-pity. Replace those negatives with peace, joy, self-control, and integrity. Success means being the best father or mother you can be. Success is sacrificing yourself emotionally to stay patient and teach your kids valuable lessons. It means being a leader (and we are all leaders) who watches someone make a mistake and learns vicariously. If they make mistakes themselves, they humbly admit to it and learn from it with a positive attitude. These characteristics make Caledonia Football amazing. It's as simple as maximizing talent. Caledonia takes average athletes and turns them into good athletes. Good athletes become great athletes, and great athletes become elite. They do this through intelligent, hard work, and a humble attitude. And, it's the average, hard-working kid that makes a great program.

All of us have a purpose. It may not be a purpose that earns us a million dollars or gets us on T.V., but we all play a role. Most of us in this country just need to realize that fulfilling our purpose is more important than being rich, popular, or famous. The part we play is being the best employee, spouse, parent, and person we can be. We aren't going to be without fault. It is sometimes messy and ugly, we all make mistakes. Simply set out to be the best person you can be and influence others to do the same. That's success. If we buy into this philosophy with all our heart, we can make a difference beyond imagination. That is the narrative that comes out of Caledonia football.

CHAPTER 2

Football is not a cure for the ills of society in and of itself. When football is used correctly, as a tool to teach and develop teenagers into young men, it can make a huge difference in the culture of a school or even an entire city. It can impact the lives of young people on a scale that few activities can. The nature of the sport is physically demanding, and as a result, it is also mentally and emotionally demanding. There is something about a sport where you have heavy physical contact that creates a bond among its participants. Football, being the ultimate team sport, creates an environment where each person is dependent on his teammates to experience success. There are no other sports like football. Yes, other sports and activities can undoubtedly impact kids and give them something to pour themselves into. Football is not for everyone, but there is something special about it.

Football, on the other hand, can easily be misused by coaches and players alike. These people create a negative reputation for the sport. Some coaches love power. They love control, and they love themselves. This is what I call negative pride and ego. It's not limited to just football. Any sport, business, or person can fall into the grips of pursuing power, control, and self-love. Since most football teams reflect the attitude of the head coach and his staff, you will often see these types of programs play dirty. They will not respect their opponent, and they are in it just for the transactional reward— winning. The lessons are wasted on them because of poor leadership.

It's also common to see programs that have a large number of kids that love to party. Drinking, smoking weed, disrespecting women, fighting, and hazing, among other negative attributes. Football tends to attract the alpha male. The alpha will tend to influence the rest of the team or organization. When this happens in the ways previously mentioned, destruction follows. These attitudes and behaviors are the false narratives preached by the world of what it means to be a man. As a result, the state of manhood in our country is a total mess. All too often, these behaviors drift into adulthood until the destruction completes itself with alcoholism, divorce, or violent crime. This is most often due to poor personal decision making and a lack of positive male leadership in the formative years and into early adulthood.

Now, it is not the job of a football staff to raise the kids in this country. That's for parents. But, when 25 percent (U.S. Census Bureau) of the households lack a male role model, coaches often inherit the job of father-figure. If the father is present, many times, he can be a negative role model. High school coaches can be fighting a battle against a negative parent and not even know it. On the flip side, great kids are usually the result of great parents. The more great kids we have on our teams, the more we can help the fringe kids who are lacking or drifting. The coaching staff can partner with these kids to create a culture of positivity and success. The job of a football coach is to invest the student-athlete and instill character in them by the time they leave their program. Not inhibit character development. Not add to the chaos. It's time for men and coaches to grow up. It's not just about football. It's about life. Maybe your life.

Caledonia football is not perfect. There are struggles within any team and school. It is nearly impossible to take a group of football kids and not have some who are participating in destructive activities outside of the team. In order to see the full impact of the program is to study where the program was.

The Dark Ages

Caledonia football in the 1980s could easily be referred to as the dark ages of the program. Alpha male dominance, fighting, bullying, hazing, alcohol, and drugs were prevalent. At that time, it was common for student-athletes at the high school to drink and smoke marijuana. This was not just a weekend or after game activity. Many of the players would smoke weed or even drink alcohol before the games. Needless to say, this was reflected poorly in the win/loss record. The football program was low-achieving despite decent talent. Excuses were used like, "We play in a tough conference." "Those schools are bigger than us." These excuses would never fly today. Caledonia is now the toughest in a tough conference, and school size doesn't matter all that much; school culture does.

In the 1980s, leadership was scarce. Jim Fruechte, Carl's younger brother, who graduated in 1988, remembers going up against seniors when he was a freshman during football practices. No doubt, the physical superiority of an 18-year-old male will dwarf that of a 14-year-old boy. Jim remembers the agony of facing these older players. Injury, concussions, tears. This was a great way by the leadership to run off young players and destroy the consistency of the program. One might say, "If they aren't tough enough to get through this, we don't want them." This was likely the attitude and a critical mistake by the coaching staff. Jim made it through. Many others did not, or they simply did not come out for football.

Greg Hoscheit, the current Caledonia football booster club president and 1984 graduate, recalled the culture. "Alcohol is just what people did. Many did drugs and smoked pot. There was fighting. Many people were known as "fighters." You just didn't mingle with the other classes. When football started, it was brutal, excessively physical, and negative."

Not only were the younger kids physically dominated on the football field, they were hazed, teased, and physically bullied off the field and in the locker room. This trickled down into the elementary school as well. Back then, the community lacked male role models to help guide the youth. As elementary school kids in the 1980s, there were few players on the teams we could genuinely look up to. The varsity coaching staff didn't spend time with young athletes. In fact, one of the football players brought the broken culture straight to my classmates.

I remember the day like it was yesterday. It was a Monday, I arrived at school a little bit early and met up with some of my fifth grade friends on the playground. We were just hanging out like any other day. My buddies started talking about their weekend. Apparently, one of their older brothers, who was on the football team, gave them alcohol. They were talking about how cool it was... in fifth grade! I knew my mom and dad would be crazy-mad if I started drinking, so I was too scared. Would I be peer-pressured to drink? What were these guys thinking? This was the beginning of a rough stretch for those friends of mine. It was magnified when we got to junior high and high school. Almost everyone drank or smoked. I needed an escape. I knew I had to avoid drinking at all costs. I needed an outlet.

In the '80s and '90s, I had an outlet. My brother Darryl loved football with a passion, and he instilled that passion in me. I remember watching and playing football since I could walk and talk. In elementary school, I discovered we could play tackle football. No, not the organized youth football leagues that you see now. It was recess ball. No pads, full contact, tackle to the ground. We started playing almost every day in first grade and concluded our recess football careers as sixth graders. Sure, we'd throw in a few days of basketball, maybe some soccer and softball from time-to-time. Perhaps once a month, we would play tag on the jungle gym, but most days, it was football.

I remember a specific day playing recess football in second grade. My friend Jeff had the ball. Two seven-year-olds were on a collision course. He wanted to score the touchdown, I wanted to bring him down. I still remember that split second before it happened. You know, how it seems in an instant, you can have a whole paragraph of thought downloaded into your brain. As we neared collision, probably in about .2 seconds, I thought to myself, "If you hit him harder than he hits you, it won't hurt as bad." So I threw my face and shoulders into his chest. I wrapped my arms around his body. The ball flew into the air. I can't remember if he cried or not after I thumped him. I distinctly remember that day. The feeling of triumph in my tackle. I became mentally tougher that day... in second grade.

People would probably cringe at this story if it happened on the playground today. They would be appalled by the violent tackle and two boys colliding at what was a high speed for a seven-year-old. I remember later that year, our second-grade teacher, Mrs. Danaher, took us outside for some extra playtime in the afternoon. The boys chose to play football— tackle, of course. The game went on for 20-30 minutes, and everyone had a blast. Then our teacher abruptly told us to come in, it was time to get back to the classroom. When we got back and settled into our desks, she told us how appalled she was that boys would play like that. So violent, so rough. She promised we would never be able to play tackle football again once she had a serious conversation with the principal.

The conversation with the principal probably didn't go her way because we played tackle football without interruption until we were in sixth grade. Then, it was finally taken away from us when David Wagner, a fifth-grader, was playing with us one day. He was running with the football and was tackled to the ground face first. David lay there in pain. We gathered round to check on him. After a few minutes, he had to be helped off the playground. Then we resumed playing the game we loved.

The next day, we learned that David had broken his collarbone. We thought injuries were part of the game. Stuff like that rarely, if ever, happened. He would heal up, and everything would be fine. What came next was devastating to both us and the school culture. Orders came over the loudspeaker, no more tackle football. What? Are they kidding? They can't keep us from playing football. Yet, the teachers and administration shut us down. We tried to ignore the rule, but the playground teachers carried out the orders. We were heart-broken. We tried playing touch football, but it wasn't the same. Soccer and basketball were not everyday sports for us. We tried, but nothing else worked. For many people, especially young boys, it is of necessity to have a physical outlet. If an energy release is not available, culture can take a turn for the worse. Football provided this type of escape. We were physical kids, and we needed a physical sport. What followed was interesting, to say the least.

What began to happen next at the elementary school was quite amazing. That's when the fighting started. Bare-knuckle, punch-in-the-face, wrestle-to-the-ground fights. It was kind of fun yet brutal at the same time. I think I got into about 10-12 fights that year. We had ranking systems, or at least some of us talked about the "rankings." The boys who won the most were ranked the highest. Lose a fight, and you'd get moved down. Not all the boys took part, of course, although most of us that had played tackle football participated. We didn't know it at the time, but fighting was our way to get that energy out. We never consciously (for the most part) went to recess thinking, "we are going to have a fight club today." No, these fights happened randomly and way more often since the football had been taken away. We had traded football for fighting. Previously, a skirmish or two would break-out every year, now fighting occurred on a weekly, sometimes daily basis.

I can't imagine what would happen if one day, people who were opposed to physical sport took organized football out of public schools altogether. They have no idea. It would be chaos. They may think that without football, wrestling, and several other sports, boys would just find a peaceful state of nirvana and slip into class, read books, smile, and be happy. Quite the opposite in my opinion. If we did not have structured sports in high school, specifically football, our system would fall apart with violence and drug abuse. As I mentioned before, football does not cure all ills. I have no doubt that a positive, character-based football program with good leadership will make school a better place. I have no doubt. I give permission to spend my hard-earned tax-payer money to do a study on that.

As a means of communication, violence carried on for my classmates and me all through school. Our class was labeled the worst in Caledonia history by some pretty tough, well-seasoned teachers. Long-time sixth-grade teachers Terry Mullins and Jeff Dahlen had seen it all. They knew all about boys. They understood the physical needs that boys have to be active, rough, and tumble.

I remember distinctly one day coming inside after recess. I had just gotten into a fight with Matt Woods, who was actually one of my best friends. He had beaten me up. I think I started crying and the whole nine yards. Mr. Mullins asked the class, "what's wrong with Mark?" Someone told him about the fight. Mr. Mullins looked at me and said, "Did you win?" I shook my head and put my eyes down toward my desk. As I looked back up at him, he said, "you gotta win those fights," and we went along with our day.

Fighting continued with us throughout high school. Some went unnoticed by school staff. A few fights outside of school were more severe, and the police got involved. I remember one day in my freshman year of high school. At lunch, I took the seat of my classmate, Brent, when he went to return his food tray. He got back to the table and wanted his place back. I said, "No way, man, I'm not moving." What happened next? Brent had a cast on his arm and used it as a weapon on my head. He whacked me hard. As he leaned over behind me, I threw my elbow into his jaw. He stared ahead, blank and dazed. I'm quite certain I concussed him. A teacher stopped by shortly after and asked if everything was ok. We said yes because neither of us wanted trouble. He ended up finding another seat, and the immediate problem went away.

Another time, I remember sitting in the stands at a varsity basketball game. I was probably a junior or senior. A kid was getting on my nerves. He was super annoying and would not stop. What was my answer? A couple punches to the face. Was it right? Absolutely not. As I reflect on those days, it was a difficult, tough culture. I regret all the fighting. However, if you weren't willing to stand up for yourself, you could get rolled over and bullied. No one was teaching boys to be men. No one was there to channel our energy and use it for good.

It wasn't just my class. When my older brother, Darryl, was in eighth grade (I was in third at that time), he was called out and challenged to an after-school fight by a dude that was bullying him and pushing for a showdown. Darryl showed up after school. So did the other kid. The other guy got his face pounded, and Darryl broke his hand in the process. He was in a cast for several weeks. Fighting was all around us. Whether on the bus, at school, after school, or at social events, it was not uncommon to witness fighting. Sadly, I did not help the situation. I just believed I was doing what I needed. I was both a bully and a victim of bullying. We all were.

On and on, I could tell story after story about fights, bullying, and hazing. Fortunately, no one was seriously hurt while we were in high school. As we got older, drug and alcohol use continued. Most of my friends that started drinking struggled throughout high school and beyond. I've lost track of most of them. Some died. Some got their heads above water and sorted out their lives. I don't really know. When I go back to Caledonia, I do not look most of those people up. This is just one person's account of what it was like back then. Everyone has a story. Many would-be similar to mine, and some would not.

Through all these years at Caledonia, there was no true male role model to put a stop to all this chaos. It was boys leading boys. Some adult men in town had good intentions. They would coach us up from time-to-time. Mostly, the adults didn't realize what was going on or just ignored it. There was no leadership. Now, when you get a high character male leader, they can't just come in and put an instant stop to the chaos. It is a process. It is not a fun process to change a deficient culture. Most give up easily, and no substantial change occurs. That did not happen in Caledonia. People were coming that would not give up. Change was coming.

CHAPTER 3

Someone had to Take the First Step

Destructive behaviors continued into 1989 until a man named Mark Froehling became head coach of Caledonia's football team, bringing with him a different approach to the game. I remember when Coach Froehling took over. He was young, probably in his late twenties. Mark was a physically strong man. He was tall with broad shoulders. Mark Froehling might be one of the nicest people I know, but he was also tough. He would bring intensity to the football field, but balance that with love off the field. Mark and his staff began diagnosing the problems associated with the program and school. "There were a lot of great people with a good community bond. Also a toughness, maybe a little roughness about many. People were not afraid to say what was on their minds. There was an undertone of acceptance for alcohol and drug use as well as some disrespectful behaviors," Froehling recalled. "It was an attitude of 'that's just what we do here.'"

Coach Froehling had an interesting journey. He was a starter on his football team in high school, although the team didn't win a single game the two years he competed on the varsity squad. Mark played a little bit in college but quickly decided to switch focus from the football field to the science fields— his eventual major. His first year at Caledonia High School, he helped coach basketball. He really didn't want to coach. "I thought I'd go to Caledonia and just teach Chemistry. I thought it would be a great gig." Froehling reflected. Somewhat reluctantly, he found himself assisting the football team his second year in 1987.

As a basketball coach, he assisted Ken Van Den Boom. A man that taught him a lot about coaching. "Ken could coach anything at a high-level," Froehling stated. "He was a great mentor." So, Mark coached basketball in his first year but then spent two seasons getting his feet wet as an assistant football coach. Following those two seasons assisting the football program, he became the next head football coach at Caledonia. "The current coach took me by the arm, walked me into the superintendent's office and said, 'Here is your next football coach.'"

Mark was not experienced as a head football coach. He really didn't quite know what to do next. But he knew he had a group of young coaches eager to learn. Mitch Mullins, Roger Knutson, and Dean Bartleson. One of the first things they did was load up in cars and head to Augustana College in Sioux Falls, South Dakota. This staff was humble and ready to learn. At Augustana, they sat with the coaching staff and learned the run and shoot offense and the 4-4 base defense. They came back to Caledonia prepared to run a practice and install scheme. The journey was about to begin.

The real question was how would they change the culture? There was substance abuse, behavior problems among players at school, and the occasional fight. Each weekend the football staff would wonder if they'd lose a player due to suspension because he was drinking or smoking. Not only that, kids were not excited to be part of the program. "There was no vision in the 80s," Carl Fruechte stated. "Kids didn't want to be a part of a negative culture where they were not treated well. The coaches were not relational." Coach Froehling concurred, "Numbers were low— not a happy atmosphere. It was a tough atmosphere. Kids were also coached down on negatively, not a lot of fun relationship type of things happening." Carl remembered being told repeatedly that his group would never amount to anything. Mark recalled a kid being kicked in the butt, literally, by a coach because he wasn't lining up correctly. The new staff understood things needed to change.

Once again, football in and of itself does not make a difference. It is part of a multi-varied solution to change the culture in our schools. However, nowhere else in a school does a group of people (the coaches) have such intimate access to a large group, specifically the perceived "alpha" male. When a coach inherits a mess, the first thing he has to do is build relationships and then call out poor behaviors and habits. This may seem obvious, but it's amazing how many programs do not address this first step. Many build the relationship but don't hold kids accountable. Some hold kids accountable, but they do not have the relationship to back it up. It's a tremendously tricky balance. Often times, the coaching staff complains when kids make mistakes. They complain about the kids, they complain about the parents, and how the world is eroding. This is a weak and indirect approach that leads to failure and apathy. The new Caledonia staff was not about to take this approach.

Coach Froehling's crew was unwavering and direct. They confronted poor behavior head-on. Difficult conversations were going to take place when it came to culture. Kids were going to be mentored but not in a weak way. The coaching staff did not want to lose the toughness; they tried to strike a balance. Froehling admits he was a bit naive at the start of his career, though. This is not an uncommon trait in young coaches. "I felt like if I pointed out the problems, alcohol is bad for you, drugs are bad for you, so just don't do it. I thought the kids would just listen and stop. I was wrong, it wasn't that easy." Coach Froehling began to understand quickly, for a kid to listen to a coach, trust had to be established. He and his staff went to work building trust and relationships.

So, the battle began. The struggle for change started. For everyone looking to take a program and turn an about-face, keep in mind, it's a battle. Sometimes it will seem like it goes backward. Sometimes you will have little victories and see change occur, but only to have that victory snatched away. The process is the most essential part. Focus on the process. Keep fighting the good fight. Never give up.

The first year of the journey ended with little change. The fall of 1989 wrapped up with just three wins and six losses. The staff understood they had their work cut out for them, and they were learning on the job. My brother Darryl's senior year was the fall of 1990. He was a talented receiver, and Joe Palen, the team's QB, had been starting since he was a freshman. Add a talented junior class, and there was potential for a successful squad. Not only that, a neighboring city, Spring Grove, had joined Caledonia as a co-op the previous year, along with their head coach, Tim Alexander, as an assistant. The chances of turning a culture around will increase dramatically when there is excitement. However, the excitement that started to emerge was to be snuffed out quickly. Joe Palen broke his hand early in the season. As is common in struggling cultures, adversity will break the will of the team. The season ended in struggle and a 2-7 record. The culture did not seem to change much. It would have been easy to quit, but the coaching staff pressed on.

The '91 season showed promise. The Warriors got off to a 5-1 start. But, when adversity came, the wheels began to fall off once again. This time in the form of a single loss. A small difficulty that leads to negative results is evidence of immaturity. Caledonia was a struggling, maturing program. The team quickly faded and lost their first playoff game. Froehling and his staff were three years in and didn't have a lot to show for their work. The battle was real. Coaches questioned if they were making a difference. Life is funny that way. We work hard at achieving our goals, we make progress, but it is so hard to see. We get tunnel vision. We are terribly hard on ourselves when we don't see results. That's the way it felt in Caledonia around this time. Progress was being made, but no one saw it. Progress is invisible at first, it cannot be measured or seen in some situations. Not even the players or coaches know when those first steps of progress are being made. Most people pack their bags and quit at this point, or in today's world, are fired after a couple of poor seasons. Fortunately, that did not happen in Caledonia. The staff stuck to it. They were in it for the long haul.

I entered the varsity program in the fall of '91 as a freshman. We would hear from Coach Froehling on occasion, but we mostly heard from our freshman coach, Carl Fruechte. We didn't know it at the time, but Carl would turn out to be one of the most successful coaches in state history. All we saw was a hard-nosed, competitive nutjob to be honest. There's no doubt about it. A lot of guys in my grade didn't like Carl as a result of his tenacity. The problem with Carl was he cared. That wasn't a problem for him, it was a problem for all the guys that didn't like him.

Keep in mind, we were labeled the worst class in Caledonia history when it came to behavior. Add in a few guys from St. Mary's, the local Catholic school that joins the public school at the ninth grade, and it was an even tougher class. Carl would battle with us but love us up at the same time. Carl's attitude was different for Caledonia at that time. Here was a guy putting down boundaries and holding us to them. He would get in your face and let you have it, but would also joke around and have fun after practice. He'd be interested in you and want the best for you.

It is challenging to describe Carl's effect on our class. Rumors were going around that he was so "clean" he'd get a buzz from Diet Coke. Not cool in a class where most drank every weekend and smoked every day. Yes, some didn't, I was one of them at that time, but the majority of the guys were into all types of stuff. Not only that, our crew followed the culture of Caledonia and the rest of the world, they treated women and girls poorly. For some reason, the girls liked the bad boys. I'll never figure that one out.

Our class was considered rough-and-tumble, many used illegal substances, and most didn't follow the rules. Kids got in trouble at school, told teachers to screw off, and womanized. Despite all of this, the coaching staff saw potential. They were not about to quit. There was some weight room presence that began before our arrival in the program. It was nowhere near where it needed to be or where it is today, but it started. They say a journey of a thousand miles begins with a single step. The journey did start. Even though we were troublemakers, many started lifting weights. We did not always know what we were doing, but we began to get a little bigger and stronger. We had learned our way around the weight room from guys like Troy Meiners and Mark Augedahl, a couple of guys that were good senior leaders on that 1991 team.

Suddenly, guys started to care a little more. That thing called progress could finally be seen— at least just a little. We were taking baby steps. The culture started to improve slowly. It was like pushing a car down a street on a snowy day. The program started moving slowly, but the traction was not good. There was a little hope, but you still had to push the car 100 yards more before you'd be somewhat safe. But at least the car was moving in the right direction, albeit slowly.

When I was a junior, a clear message came through to everyone that the coaches in Caledonia were serious about taking a stand. Froehling started the LIFT program. It stood for "Leading into the Future Together." If someone wanted to be a captain of any sport, they had to be a part of this program. We all signed eligibility forms with the state high school league agreeing to their substance guidelines. But to join this group, you had to make a pledge. You had to give your word. No drugs or alcohol. As part of the LIFT program, we also attended an annual retreat led by Rob Kesselring. We bonded through sharing stories, outdoor group activities, and learning how to lead and stand up for what's right. It was a great group while it lasted, and it helped send a message to all the athletes. If you are going to be in athletics, you are going to make a commitment not to use alcohol, drugs, or tobacco. The standard was set, the culture needed to change.

By the time I became a senior, there was more improvement. We were doing some training and working out. Several guys would come to the school for lifting and running. It wasn't much, but at least it was something. The needle was moving in the correct direction. Then I noticed something amazing. The guys started talking about giving up drinking and smoking for the season. Just a decade earlier, players were smoking weed before games. Now, there was some type of sacrifice brewing. I'll give up this (drinking) to get a result (the best chance of winning). It was this season that Coach Froehling decided to make it fully intentional to teach character. Mostly because of the lack of it between my classmates and me. They were a little wild and crazy, and I was self-centered. Neither helps a program win.

The Book

A lot of coaches would think it is weird. Coach Froehling had full support from his staff. They knew what they were up against. Perhaps this group of coaches started to feel a change rising, but understood there was still a long road ahead. That is why we read a book called "The Right Kind of Hero's." It was the story of Bob Shannon, a high school football coach in East St. Louis. The culture in Caledonia was not as bad as East St. Louis. Not by a longshot. However, the book gave the coaching staff hope. If change can occur in East St. Louis, change can occur in Caledonia. As a result, Coach Froehling started to read to us. We called it "storytime." No, the reading was not before or after practice in some meeting room. Coach read to us right there on the practice field, right in the middle of practice. Helmets, shoulder pads, and all. We would get a comfortable spot on the grass, take a nice break from the labor of football, relax, and listen. It was a story of hope. It was a story of change. If you ask any of the football players that were there in the fall of '94, they will remember storytime.

When change needs to occur, the fastest way is through the heart. Like Mark thought in his early years, most believe it's all about a mental understanding. If you understand something is bad, I tell you to stop doing it, and you stop doing it. Wrong. The way to change a human being is through the heart. It is about showing them the qualities we want you to adopt are important enough that we will stop football practice and explain them to you. We care about you and this team more than anything else. This is the message that was directly and indirectly sent by this simple concept of reading a book about hope and change. That, along with role-modeling. You can say what you want about that coaching staff, they were young and inexperienced, but they lived life the right way. We knew they role-modeled what they were preaching to us, and we respected that.

Our class had a strong bond. I think it was formed from being under the tyranny of the class that went before us. They were as tough as we were, maybe more destructive. The behavior of our group somehow got more attention than the jerks who were one year older than us. I felt like I was constantly bullied by the class of '94 in some way, shape, or form. I'm quite sure my friends Matt Woods, Jared Hickey, and I were the target of a lot of this bullying because we weren't drinking. However, I am certain many other classmates felt the same way. Our bond was the result of this oppression.

The book, the leadership, and the attempts to change the culture strengthened that bond. I even started to feel a little love for the guys next to me. I began to trust. Others were feeling the same thing. We were taking this seriously. The team was excited, and we had a good amount of talent. We were ready for our senior year. More prepared than any Caledonia team of the past two decades.

CHAPTER 4

"Being in a battle together creates a much greater bond than sitting in a chemistry class. The culture of sport can make a difference. It's an extension of the classroom" -Coach Mark Froehling.

We were tough kids. Tough and mean. Coach Froehling wanted us to be tough and nice. In the fall of 1994, most of us were not quite able to put nice with tough. In the words of our coach: "Some people were just naturally tough. Some guys were just going to give people a huge lick. I wanted people tough because they cared, not just because they were mean. How much more will you sacrifice for someone you love? That guy next to me needs me to be really good. I'm going to block that guy better than I ever could. I'm gonna put a lick on this guy because my team needs me. I'm going to be good because my team needs me to be good. I'm not doing this for accolades. I'm doing this for the team."

Even though tough and nice did not completely line up the way Coach wanted it to, the team was making progress. We entered the season with optimism and promise. Our class was excited. As the August heat and humidity set in, fall camp was ready to begin. "The Right Kind of Heroes" started during two-a-days. At first, when Coach started reading to us, we were just happy to get a break during practice. Most people think it's always 40 degrees or less in Minnesota. Actually, we get the best of both worlds. It can be 100 degrees and humid in the summer, negative 60-degree wind chills in the winter, and everything in between. I like it. It's a nice variety and creates toughness. All that said, the character-building started taking place on the football field. Our class worked hard during two-a-days. We attacked conditioning and paid attention to the details being taught at practice. There was a different feel. There was a sense of enjoyment. We were glad to be at practice. The past few years we had dreaded it... probably because, as seniors, we were finally the team leaders.

The first game against La Crescent closed in quickly. La Crescent was a rival town about twenty minutes from Caledonia. They had throttled us the year before on our field. Now, it was time to go to their place. Anxiety built as the lights flipped on before the game. Our group of seniors had bonded. We were in charge of this team. The coaches had our respect, and a sense of unity and love began to build. I was obsessed with rushing for 125 yards that game. As a running back, my goal was to rush for 1,000 yards in the first eight games. This was no doubt a sign of my immaturity and selfishness, but my attitude would soon change.

We took the ball early in the first quarter and marched down the field. Jed Hammell, our talented quarterback, scored the first touchdown. I felt great ripping off a run of over 20 yards. The game was tight, tied 7-7 at halftime. Jed also returned kickoffs. He grabbed the opening kickoff of the second half and ran it back for a touchdown giving us the lead. Jed continued to lead the team, as he would all year, by adding a third touchdown that game. My heart began to change during that game. I had so much fun just winning that I forgot about my goal and started to focus on the team first. I was pleased to add a few tough first down runs at the end of the game to seal the victory. We won 21-7. Jed was no doubt the star, but he was a humble kid, and that served our team well. This allowed our team to bond even further. Winning was more important than any one player now.

Southland was our next game. They were a class smaller than us but a tough football school at that time. They were ranked in the top 10 in the state of Minnesota. It was a hot, humid September day in Caledonia. The heat was oppressive, probably 90 degrees with a heat index close to 100. I remember Coach Froehling stressed to us the importance of drinking plenty of water. In small school football, teams do not have the luxury of playing kids on only one side of the football. In many cases, the players need to be on offense, defense, and special teams.

As game time approached and we settled in, the sun started to set, and heat lightning lined the eastern sky. It was a beautiful sight. When you are playing in a football game, it seems like you are in a different world. Time and space tend to disappear as you enter another dimension. The lightning to the east was something I noted as a brutal battle between two football teams began. It was an escape. But I quickly refocused, I didn't want to escape. I wanted to fight and win.

The game was low scoring. The heat was intense, but ignored, at least by our team. The grit and tenacity that solidified in us through August practice and our week one win came out on the field that night. This is the first time I remember feeling true unity with a group of men. Our unstated communication said in our hearts, "You can bring the heat, you can hit us or even hurt us, but we will never quit, ever." For me, this was tested in the first half. I remember our quarterback Jed ran an option play to the right side of the field, toward Southland's sideline. He was running east/west (that's sideways) and was forced to pitch the ball. I was his option-man. As the ball floated through the air, I watched into my hands; at the same time, I knew Brandon Voight, Southland's explosive safety and running back, was bearing down on me hard. As soon as I caught the ball, CRACK! Brandon's helmet went right into my facemask. I puked in my mouth then swallowed it. I got up and stumbled a bit as I made my way back to the huddle. "You all right Esch?" Matt Woods asked ironically, he was the kid who beat me up in sixth grade. "I'm good," I replied. The next play was called, and we broke the huddle. My job was to block the outside linebacker. As I got down in my stance, I peeked at him. To my surprise, there were two of him! Then one, then two, then one! I didn't even think about it, but I had been concussed for sure. I was watching this guy with a split vision. I didn't care, I had a job to do. As the ball snapped, I attacked him, when he became one again, I exploded into him and crushed him. My vision returned to normal. I wasn't going to quit. Neither was anyone else.

The hot, physical game continued into the fourth quarter. We were down on the scoreboard and needed to get into the end-zone for the win. Our entire team was exhausted, I am sure Southland was too, but our resolve to win this game did not diminish. We took the ball and drove down the field. The tension rose, and our anxiety level was high. The stress created in a tight football game is tremendous, yet it allows kids to learn how to focus and step up when needed. We methodically moved the ball down the field toward the end zone. On a critical fourth and 4, we ran the same option play I mentioned earlier. This time I took the pitch from Jed and ripped off enough yardage for the first down. Shortly after that, Jed put it in the end zone again, and we went on to win the game. We started the season 2-0.

The next four games flew by. We won them all. Week three, we barely escaped against Mable-Canton. We scored a touchdown and a two-point conversion to win the game with less than a minute left. Situations like this build character. The old quote, "You can learn more on the 2-yard line than you can anywhere else in life," means you need to do hard things. Those hard things will suck. You'll think you can't do it. You'll think about quitting. Then you will breakthrough. That makes you better. These situations build character, teamwork, and strengthen the bond of a group of men.

After six weeks, our team was 6-0. Undefeated going into a week seven match-up with Lanesboro, a small town in southeast Minnesota. That team was loaded with talent. The tension between two undefeated teams competing was palpable. I remember seeing Coach Froehling sitting in front of the school a few hours before game time. He looked as serious as I had ever seen him. Coach had an intense look in his eyes. Perhaps he was thinking back to 1991. Just four years prior, that team lost the big game, and the season pummeled out of control. Winning increases buy-in, there is no doubt, and winning this game would allow this coaching staff to teach the culture of character at an even higher level.

We were focused and unified. We were bonded through the fire. We were confident, and we knew we would not back down. Butterflies flew through stomachs, and intensity glared through our eyes as we entered the field for kickoff. What followed was a fierce battle. No one backed down. Early on, it was a scoreless game. Each team moved the ball, each team was stopped. I never ran so hard in my life. All I remember from that game is how each play felt like it could make the entire game. You just didn't know when that play would happen. The battle raged to a scoreless pause at halftime. We fought, scratched, and clawed but fell behind by two scores going into the fourth quarter. We closed it to a one-score game, but Lanesboro sealed the deal with a touchdown in the last few minutes. We lost the game by two touchdowns.

The loss was heartbreaking. People wondered if the wheels would fall off the bus as they did just a few years prior. We had one more game against a weak opponent, then we'd enter our section play, which was considerably tougher than our conference schedule. We would play Hiawatha Valley teams. The Hiawatha Valley league was our regular season in previous years. We now played in the Southeast Conference. The guys who graduated in the years prior to us made it clear they thought our success was simply because of our schedule. We disagreed. But, we knew the real test would come in the playoffs. We crushed our last regular-season opponent and headed into section playoffs.

CHAPTER 5

The Playoffs Begin

"Look at them!" I said in a team huddle right after halftime. I was pointing to seniors watching the game from the class of '92 who had fallen apart after one loss in the regular season. "Look at them! If we lose this game, we are no better than they were! It's time to step up!" We were struggling against the #7 seed Lake City on our own field. We were the #2 seed. If we lost this game, no doubt we'd be targeted by that class of former Warriors. "We told you that your schedule was easy," they would say— most of them were still around town. We respected them, but the thought of them ribbing us was unbearable. We had to get it going.

The problem was we kept turning the ball over. We had six turnovers in the game. Match that with significant penalties, and we were in the hole 7-6 in the fourth quarter. Lake City had a big, strong running back/linebacker. He was tough. I had to block him late in the third quarter on my assignment. I put a decent lick on him, but he absorbed it well. He looked at me as he helped me up off the grass, "Man, your team hits hard. Your team hits really hard." I thanked him and ran back to the huddle. We did hit hard. We were Caledonia kids.

Late in the fourth quarter, less than two minutes left. We had the ball, still down 7-6. There was a pit in my stomach. I'm sure everyone else's belly, too. Time was running out. Would our successful season end with a first-round playoff loss like almost all the previous years? We had the ball, and we were heading toward the Lake City goal line, but things looked bleak. One of our teammates, an offensive lineman, fell to the ground after a play and started crying. Adam Augedahl, maybe the toughest kid on the team, kicked him and yelled, "Get up!" Not the best way to motivate, but it worked. The kid got up and rejoined the huddle.

It was third and about six with time running out. I remember taking a handoff and bolting around the left end with the ball. I sprinted as fast as I could, past the first-down marker. There, waiting to tackle me, was that big linebacker. I put my shoulder down, just like I did in second grade, and hit him harder than he hit me. Thump! He flew backward, and I went flying out of bounds. First down!

We moved the ball down to about the 20-yard line. I remember it was fourth and 6. Coach Froehling called a timeout with just over a minute left in the game. The sideline conversation was intense. The coaches settled on an option play to the left. That meant it would be either me or Jed, our talented running quarterback that would have the ball in our hands. As we lined up, the nervousness disappeared. Our team thought only about winning the football game. Alcohol and drugs were not needed. Football was our drug.

As the ball was snapped, Jed ran to his left. I was running with him in what we call pitch relationship, ready to get the ball if needed. Jed looked like he was going to pitch it to me, I was ready, but he faked the pitch and turned upfield. He bolted the 6 yards needed for the first down and kept going. A talented runner and a physical kid, Jed made several moves and chugged towards the end zone. I put my hands up about 20 yards behind him. As he sprinted across the goal line for the game-winning touchdown, I fell to the ground with a spirit of gratitude. It was the winning touchdown! We had won a playoff game! We finished out the last minute of the game, holding on to the lead. We were exhausted. One of the greatest feelings in life is being tired after a hard-fought victory. That feeling is something I miss to this day. We earned the win and would play the following Saturday at home against Pine Island.

One playoff win set the town abuzz with excitement. There was a big crowd at the first playoff game. Now this one showed promise for a large turnout as well because we had a beautiful October afternoon to play football. There was a coolness in the air, but the weather was warm enough for a t-shirt. It was a great day, and the game ended with the perfect outcome. Behind stout defensive play and a ball-control offense, we pulled off the win by three scores. One of the highlights of my football career is scoring the last touchdown of that game. It was a run of about 30 yards to seal the victory. When we watched the film, you could hear Ken Vanden Boom yell, "I love it!" as the touchdown was scored. The day was amazing. I later found out a good number of my teammates celebrated by driving the back-roads, smoking cigarettes, and drinking some beer. The culture was better but far from over the hump.

The following week Caledonia played in it's first-ever section championship. We took a bus trip about 75 minutes north to Zumbrota-Mazeppa to meet a talented team led by senior running back Brad Prigge. He was a tough and fast running back on a talented team. We got off to a slow start in that game. The Cougars went up 7-0 early and controlled the line of scrimmage. They physically dominated our team. We were tough, but they were tough, fast, and strong. That was the difference. Zumbrota led by three touchdowns late in the fourth. We never quit and scored a touchdown late, but it was evident that we were going to lose. Tears started to stream down our faces as we realized our high school football careers were coming to an end. For most kids, they would never play the game again, at least not with pads. Maybe a college flag football league would be in their football future. Organized football was over.

Somewhere in the crowd during the game was a man by the name of Ernie Hodges. He watched as we were physically dominated by Zumbrota. He had been following Caledonia football for years. He felt he had something to offer the program. Having a weight training background, he knew that a good weight program could help our team. No one knew it, but that man was about to change the trajectory of Caledonia football.

CHAPTER 6

Ernie Hodges

Ernie drove home by himself after that loss to Zumbrota in the fall of 1994. His stepson, Jesse, participated in the football program at the lower levels. Jesse's seventh and eighth-grade coaches, Kris Fadness and Terry Mullins, were okay with Ernie coming around and watching practice. They eventually developed a relationship and learned about his background in the weight room, which led to a couple of kids on that team going to his house and working out in his garage. Caledonia was about to learn how to squat.

A seventh-grade player, Mitch Schiltz, was the first to get to Ernie's garage. Mitch's dad spoke with Ernie and set up the workout times for him. Soon after Jesse Nelson (name changed due to active SEAL duty), came in and started to learn. Jesse's dad came by to make sure Ernie was on the up and up. Then the workouts commenced. Eventually, Kris invited Ernie to a Sunday night open gym session at the high school. Kids and adults would play basketball, and some would go on the stage of the gym where the weights were and work out.

This is where Ernie met Mark Froehling. Mark talked with him about his background, and Ernie offered to put a program together for the team. All he wanted in return was a spot on the sideline Friday nights to watch the game. "I hated watching games from anywhere but the sideline," Ernie said. Mark invited Ernie over to his house a few times to visit. Consider it the '90s version of our current background check system. Mark deemed Ernie a good guy and set him up with the team for a meeting.

The first meeting took place in Roger Knutson's science room. Mark introduced Ernie, and he shared some thoughts. "Well....there are 8 teams left in the state of Minnesota, and you ain't one of them." That's what Ernie told the kids he was meeting with from the class of '96. Ernie continued to challenge the kids and painted a vision for what the program would do. At this point, it would be great to say the rest was history, but that was not the case.

What followed was frustrating for Ernie and the coaching staff. Even though he was putting a system in place, there was not much buy-in happening. Kids were just not used to getting to the weight room. To complicate the situation, the weight room was on the stage in the gym. It would be shut down for any event that took place on the stage, so kids had limited access. It made it hard to develop consistency. It was challenging to get the momentum going. A lot of coaches give up at this point. Once again, many coaches just blame it on the kids, parents, or the distractions of the town. Not Mark, Ernie, or this Caledonia staff. They were determined to figure this thing out.

Coach Froehling saw the need for a new facility. He sought out the approval of the superintendent for an idea he had to build a new weight room facility. The administration told him if he could raise funds, he could build a small building off the back of the school. So Mark went to work. He saw the potential for increasing the weight room attendance because he had access to Ernie and his expertise. He just needed the building. Mark went to local service clubs and raised about $15,000. Not enough to build, but the community rallied around the project. Local building companies offered free labor. Local stores offered building material, a furnace, and carpet at cost. The crews went to work nights and weekends, evidence of community support, and the ability to rally when needed. Before long, there was a brand new weight room. Not the fancy, high-end weight rooms you see in many high schools today, this was a basic but functional room that kids could use effectively. Finally, there was a space athlete's could use to get better. But the next lesson that Caledonia would have to learn was patience.

"I need more kids in the weight room." Ernie would say. "There should be way more kids buying in." Ernie wanted all the kids, but even with the new weight room, most kids were avoiding the work. Ernie knew of more kids that should be involved. The football program continued the next two seasons under the direction of Mark Froehling. Things were improving, but not as quickly as everyone had hoped. The program was not able to get over the hump, win the football section, and get into the state playoffs. Still, Ernie, Mark, and the coaching staff continued to work. They were always trying to improve.

Even with a new direction, a new room for workouts, and some increased success, attendance was average at best. The environment was better than it had been in the '80s, but there was still something missing. The program needed a breakout win, something to push the momentum over the top. The program needed something to celebrate. It was a constant struggle. The drinking, drug, and fighting culture had improved, but it was still there and negatively impacted the program at times.

I didn't meet Ernie Hodges until after my high school football career ended. However, I was one of the first people to latch on to his philosophies. I was looking for something since my football career was over. I reluctantly gave up the pursuit of a college football career because I had been accepted into a highly competitive athletic training program at the University of Wisconsin-La Crosse. I still wanted to work out in Caledonia, and Ernie was a guy I wanted to be around; tough, honest, and to the point. Ernie didn't use high energy to get the best out of you. Ernie would get the best out of you by simple, yet compelling challenges. He had a southern drawl and backed up his talk with his strength in the weight room. Ernie would work out with us on occasion and show us what it was like to move the real weight. We all wanted to be that strong. Caledonia just needed more high school kids to have the desire to get better.

Lake City, October 1996

One Friday night in the fall of '96, the Warriors traveled to Lake City to take on the Tigers. Just two years earlier, Lake City was their first playoff win since 1986. The rain came down in sheets, and the field was a mess. Caledonia came out of the gate flat. The game was like a lion fighting a sheep. The sheep wanted nothing to do with the lion. Lake City crushed Caledonia that night. In a rain-soaked, mud-filled game, the Warriors of Caledonia ended their season with an embarrassing 33-0 loss to Lake City, finishing 4-5 overall. It was a step backward for the program. After the game, the team loaded up the bus and headed home while a few of the coaches went to a gas station in town before driving home for the night. An older gentleman came up to the coaches and asked, "Are you the assistant coaches for Caledonia?" Coach Fruechte answered, "Yes sir, we are." "Your boys didn't want to be out on that field tonight, did they?" the man asked. "No sir, they didn't,"

Carl responded. This was the last game Mark Froehling would coach in Caledonia. This was the night Carl Fruechte vowed to himself that an embarrassment like this could never be allowed to happen again.

A New Life

Mark and Lori Froehling were feeling the pressure to make a decision. Was it time to put down roots in Caledonia? Or, was it possible to move a few hours north and settle down with their three children and be closer to extended family? It was a difficult decision, and not one that was taken lightly. "These coaches were my friends, we had a great group of young coaches. We not only worked together, but we did life together," recalled Coach Froehling. The couple had a difficult decision to make.

Thoughts of moving further north became more real when a teaching job opened at Farmington High School. Farmington is located 30 miles south of the Minneapolis/St. Paul metro area. The move would bring both Mark and his wife, Lori, closer to family. So Mark applied for the job and accepted their offer. It was an emotional time. They had spent a decade in Caledonia—a decade of building relationships. The staff had fought vigorously to improve the culture of the program and the school. It wasn't easy to just pick up and go. But, there was also relief. It may be difficult to understand, but giving up the responsibility as a head football coach was also a release. There is great responsibility that goes along with this role. It is hard to explain the burden of being a head football coach, especially in the state of Minnesota. A coach earns approximately $5,000 a year, and they carry a year-long commitment. A coach is always available for his players, helps year-round in the weight room, is constantly battling to get kids out for football, and the summer included practices and even scrimmages. It was a workload Mark Froehling was ready to give up. He improved the program as much as he could. He dug the program out of the pit and started to build something positive. It was time to move on. "It was almost a relief to move on, but it was hard to leave the community," Mark said. His next move? Go into the athletic director's office and recommend Carl Fruechte as the next head coach. "Looking back, God had a plan in all this. I left at just the right time, and Carl stepped into the role that was intended for him. It worked out perfectly."

CHAPTER 7

I was hanging around the workshop at Ma Cal Grove Country Club in Caledonia. I spent ten summers working there as a member of the grounds crew. Ken Vanden Boom, Caledonia's athletic director, came walking up with his golf clubs. This was not uncommon. Ken was a golf enthusiast and also built a dominant girls golf program at Caledonia High School. "I heard you are looking for a football coach," I shouted from about 20 yards away. He responded, "Yes, we are, you have any suggestions?" I answered confidently, "I think Carl Fruechte would be an outstanding head coach!" Now, I don't think the opinion of a 20-year-old carried a lot of weight, but I remember that day because I was actually asked for my opinion. Whoever took the job, Ken thought it would be tough for the team to win a game the upcoming season.

Carl was named head football coach that summer. It was something he dreamed about since he was in high school. But was he ready for the job? He admits he could have been an assistant coach under Mark Froehling for the rest of his life. Mark was building character in the program. Everything seemed to be moving in the right general direction despite the 1996 season and the tough loss to Lake City. Coach Froehling was gone, and Carl was up for the challenge. The staff was bolstered by new assistant coach Mike Schafer who would run the defense. Add to that a three-year starting quarterback in John Hauser; Mitch Schiltz, who had been training with Ernie for years; in addition, two talented athletes in the backfield, Kurt Lange and future SEAL Jesse Nelson.

Things started to change immediately when Coach Fruechte took over, quite simply, he was more aggressive in his approach than most high school coaches. Carl started reaching out to his players—meeting with them one-on-one. He even called up Johny Hauser, his returning quarterback, and took him to breakfast in La Crosse. "I was excited when Carl was hired," recalled John Hauser. "I remember that first breakfast we had together— his passion was going to be Caledonia football. There was no doubt." Carl wanted to know what was going on inside the program at the player level. He valued each player and wanted to create the best atmosphere possible. Carl wanted their opinions on what needed to be done and what they'd like to see done in the program. This gave the returning players a sense of belonging right away. Working with Ernie, Carl became an ardent salesman of the weight room.

With a new intensity and focus came pushback from some of the players and community. Carl said he was too focused or too naive to know it was going on, and if he did, he would just ignore it. "It's all about sports with this guy." "There's more to life than football," came the grumbling from some teachers, parents, and community members. Some of the players also gave pushback. They didn't want to spend all their time in the weight room or working on football. They wanted to have jobs, make money, and enjoy themselves. Carl had to help these kids see that they could get their workouts in, have a job, and find downtime. The key was the kids seeing value in "why" they'd want to do something like this; what would be the payoff? Carl truly didn't realize there was backlash taking place until Jack Hauser (John's Dad) came up to him one day and said, "Carl, I've got your back. Don't worry." This caught Carl off guard. He thanked Jack, but he remembered thinking that people must be talking him down, but Carl didn't care. He had a program to build.

One of the first things Carl changed is how teammates treat each other. Again, as we learned from Coach Froehling's tenure, change is never immediate. Change requires constant encouragement and role-modeling. Coach Fruechte immediately began to preach that Caledonia was one team. He attended every lower-level football game he could. If the team was traveling, he would have the coach call him after the game, give him the score and update him on how they performed. Carl was invested in the entire football program; as a result, the players saw this and followed suit.

The seniors were a group of nice kids, but they didn't have the brotherhood that is required to make deep playoff runs. They performed well during the season, going 6-2 and headed into the playoffs with confidence. After a first-round win, the team headed to Dover-Eyota for the section semi-final game. I distinctly remember this game. My brother Darryl and cousin Chris Zaiger drove down from the

Minneapolis area and joined the team on the sideline. I knew these kids well after training with many of them in Ernie's garage for a few years, this included Mitch Schiltz, the first to hit Ernie's garage. I would later coach against Mitch when I was at Mankato West. Regardless, I felt connected to this team and certainly to Carl and Ernie. The Warriors aired it out early and took a decent lead. However, Dover-Eyota stormed back and ended the Warriors season with a victory.

The next year the Warriors lost a talented group of seniors. But they reloaded the team with skilled players. With a few more kids in the weight room, the 1998 team ripped off eight wins in a row to start. The one-two punch of Jesse Nelson and Kurt Lange was tough to contain. Add in Ernie Hodges stepson Jesse, a formidable lineman, and the Warriors were tough. Having raced to that 8-0 start in '98-—the first in decades—the town began to show more support for Carl's philosophies. But how the season ended was tough to handle. Jesse Worsely and Jesse Nelson were both out with major injuries, and unfortunately, the Warriors fell in the first round of the playoffs. A disappointing end to one of the most successful regular seasons ever. Coaches cannot control injuries, and injuries had affected this season dramatically.

CHAPTER 8

The Philosophy

In the winter of 2001, Coach Fruechte sat in the locker room office at the old Caledonia High School, frustrated, sad, and a little angry. He had dedicated years of pouring his heart and soul into the program— doing all the things he thought necessary to win and be more successful each year—but still only getting 5-7 kids in the weight room at a time. Ernie was always frustrated with the numbers, and he'd let Carl know about it. "If you get me the kids, I'll make them stronger," Ernie would say. Carl knew this. He didn't need anyone else to tell him. Thus, a slight depression fell on Carl. It was a low point. "I wasn't clinically depressed, but it was a hard time for me. I would call it a time of despair," he said. Looking at Carl, you would never know that this type of thing could happen to him. He's always positive and upbeat, kind and polite. Despair happens to everyone in this world. It is something to be endured and fought through for all of us at different points in our lives. We must be patient in times of affliction. Patience was never one of Carl's strengths. He wants things to happen and happen right now. "Why am I only getting a few kids to follow me? What am I doing wrong?" Carl broke down emotionally when he was by himself at the school. But a breakthrough was coming...

The Breakthrough

Oftentimes as coaches, we tend to think it's about us. We can wallow in self-pity. It's not about you. Or in Carl's words to himself, "It's not about you dummy." Broken down, stripped of pride or ego, questioning why kids were not following him like he thought they should— this is the phrase that was downloaded into his thoughts. Carl grew up with parents who believed in Jesus Christ and taught him the lessons of the greatest and most influential leader in history. Did his faith wander from time to time? Like most people, yes, it did. Carl would admit that he lost focus on his faith and felt like he was doing everything on his own. "I got caught up in winning—it was what I wanted most—but God spoke to me that day, and that's when everything started to change. I started to give it all to Him." During his time of despair in the locker room, Carl had been thinking about the great coaches in the game of football, "What would they do if they were in my position?" The answer came through a voice in his head. "The Holy Spirit spoke to me that day. The greatest leader of all time, Jesus Christ, didn't get everyone to follow him. Why should I worry about trying to get everyone to follow me? I decided my priority would be building up young men of character and integrity." This was when everything started to change for Carl and Caledonia football. Carl had built young men of character and integrity before, but now he was doing it with the right frame of mind and with his heart in the proper place. He wasn't here to build wins, he was here to grow the players into men. There was no immediate breakthrough in the win-loss column, but Carl felt rejuvenated after he committed it all to God.

Brent Schroeder joined the staff in 2001. Brent graduated the same year I did in 1995. Brent left college before he had completed his degree in school psychology. He was running a landscaping business in the Caledonia area and had been coaching at the eighth-grade level. Brent vividly remembered the fantastic season the Warriors put together our senior year. His high school football experience is what drove him to coach. Brent was hungry to give the kids the best possible experience, no matter what. The Warriors won seven regular-season games in his first year running the defense. But the playoffs seemed to be a stumbling block for the program once again. Caledonia had never won more than two playoff games, and 2001 would be no different. The Warriors lost a heart-breaker to Plainview-Elgin-Millville (PEM) 21-20 to end the season 7-2.

The next two seasons were the worst Carl had witnessed as far as winning, but the team was facing tougher opponents. Caledonia switched from the Southeast Conference to the Three Rivers Conference. Those two seasons may not have been what Carl and his staff were looking for when it came to wins, but it allowed the program to see what they needed to do to compete at the highest level in the state. It was also a great test for Carl to focus more and more on his faith during this process. These years indeed were years of growth for the Warriors— in all areas. Caledonia ended the '02 season with a 5-4 record after losing to Lake City once again.

The 2003 season was just above average by winning percentage. Caledonia started the season scoreless in the first two games. They snuck out a few victories to finish the regular season 4-4. No one expects greatness to appear after a 4-4 season; usually, 4-4 seasons end in the playoffs as they did in the regular-season—average. Carl Fruechte remembers going to the section seeding meeting and receiving the #5 seed. But even more vivid is the Lake City coach going up to Bill Ihrke, then head coach at Plainview-Elgin-Millville, and telling him they looked forward to playing them in the second round of the section playoffs. Carl overheard this conversation and started steaming. Lake City was the #4 seed and would host Caledonia in just a few days. What business did this coach have telling Plainview they would see them in the next round. Were they assuming a victory over Caledonia?

This was the fuel Carl used to fire up his team. Lake City was confident they'd beat Caledonia. The Saturday practice locked the Warriors in with the playoff game was just a few days away. On Tuesday, the team loaded the bus and headed north to Lake City, located on Lake Pepin, which is part of the Mississippi River. It's a beautiful small town in Southeast Minnesota. However, Carl and his Warriors were not there to take in the view. Unlike years before, this Caledonia team was locked and loaded, ready for battle. The worst thing an opposing team can do is disrespect another team. In some cases, a superior team can disrespect an inferior team and get away with it. This was not the case. What followed was a dismantling of the Lake City Tigers. The Warriors, led offensively by quarterback Casey Meiners and running back Lee Rohrer, both tough and talented boys from neighboring Brownsville, crushed the Tigers. Never again would Caledonia lose to Lake City.

The Plainview-Elgin-Millville game was a Saturday night game on a cold October night. Rain turned to snow periodically during the game. PEM was on a twenty-plus game winning streak and the defending state champions. Earlier that season, they shut out Caledonia 14-0. Carl's coaching staff talked all week to the kids about how they had as good a chance as anyone at ending the streak. They preached, "We have them where we want them, and we are the underdog with nothing to lose." The game did not disappoint. What followed was an all-out war.

A year earlier, I sat with Carl in the bleachers of the Metrodome as we watched Plainview-Elgin-Millville win the state championship. "I'll be right back, I want to go grab Coach Ihrke and congratulate him," Carl told me. He had a ton of respect for Bill Ihrke, and Bill saw Carl and Caledonia as an up and coming program. There was mutual respect between the two teams. PEM respected Caledonia, and Caledonia respected PEM. Carl Fruechte and Bill Ihrke had become good friends. The stage was set for an epic high school football battle. On a cold, rainy Minnesota night, the game commenced and turned quickly into a defensive struggle. The teams exchanged punts, and tough hits the entire first half. Caledonia just barely squeaked out a halftime lead 3-0.

Shutting out Plainview was an accomplishment of a stout defense led by Josh Meyer, Nathan Becker, and up and coming sophomore and future NFL football player Karl Klug. Klug barely recalled the game, "As a sophomore, I didn't pay much attention to how good PEM was. I don't think I played all that great." Coach Fruechte told a different story. "I talked with Bill Ihrke at a clinic after the season was over. He told me they could not find an answer for Karl Klug. Plainview put their best offensive tackle on him to no avail." At halftime, Coach Ihrke asked his senior offensive lineman if he could block Klug in the second half. His best lineman told him, "No, I can't handle him. He's too good." In a split second, Bill had to decide whether to light a fire under his player or change his game plan. He chose to change his game plan. Meantime, in the Caledonia locker room, Carl Fruechte told his team, "We have them right where we want them."

The defensive battle continued in the second half. Meiners and Rohrer were held in check for the most part, and the teams traded punts and played a field position football game. This is the way the game played out until a critical play early in the fourth quarter. "I remember it like it was yesterday," said Brent Schroeder. "I called a fire blitz off the weak side on a key down." Defensive tackle Nathan Becker broke through for a big hit. The ball shot into the air, and Josh Meyer snatched it and raced around sixty-yards for a huge defensive score and a gigantic momentum swing. The scoop and score drill that the Warriors methodically practice every day as part of their warm-up paid off big time. Caledonia kicked the extra point to make it a two-score game at 10-0. The winning streak for PEM was in serious jeopardy.

Mid-fourth quarter PEM took possession of the football in their own territory. They needed to score quickly and get the ball back for a chance to win. However, the Caledonia staff coached their kids up to keep the ball inbounds whenever possible. The team was taught to tackle the ball carrier or receiver quickly to keep the clock running. This proved to be a great strategy. It is called the four-minute defense. Keep the offense in-bounds—preventing the big play—and keep the clock going. PEM did methodically move the ball, but it ended up being to Caledonia's advantage. PEM drove the ball down to the ten-yard line of Caledonia and threatened to score, but it was at the expense of time. The drive lasted about 5-6 minutes and was extinguishing hope for the Bulldogs. On a critical fourth down from the 10-yard line, Caledonia was called for a pass interference call in the end zone. The penalty just ended up burning more time off the clock. PEM eventually punched it in, but it was too late. The Warriors recovered an onside kick attempt by PEM, and the clock ran out. Caledonia shocked the state of Minnesota by knocking off the number one team. The entire sideline was ecstatic as time ran out. "We weren't supposed to win that game," Schroeder said. Coach Fruchte proudly recalled that game, "This was a program-changing win for us."

The following week the Warriors traveled to Byron for the section championship. A game they had never won in program history. "It was one of the coldest games I remember playing in," said Karl Klug. The wind, rain and eventually snow made the mid-30 degree temperature seem even colder. Exhausted and banged up from an emotional season and hard-hitting physical playoff games, the Warriors once again failed to win a section championship. They lost a battle 17-7. "We just didn't have anything left in our tanks, we were extremely proud of that group of kids, they played their hearts out," said Coach Fruechte. The Warriors finished the season 6-5, but their confidence was bolstered, and they returned a good amount of young talent.

The following year the Warriors capitalized on their momentum from the fall of 2003. They finished the regular season 7-1. Their only loss was to PEM, and the Warriors had won their first two playoff games. This put them right back into the section championship game with a chance to go to the state tournament. This time, the number one ranked team Kasson-Mantorville stood in their way. Kasson-

Mantorville was similar to Caledonia, always fielding reliable, tough, and strong kids. Kasson-Mantorville is a small community, just a short drive from Rochester, Minnesota—home to the world-renowned Mayo Clinic. K-M, mostly known for its wrestling program, transferred that wrestling toughness and grit onto the football field most years. In 2004, they boasted the number one team in the state.

Caledonia football was turning into a team known for its own tough, strong, and fast kids. Ernie Hodges was beginning to gain momentum in the weight room. Numbers were increasing, and Coach Fruechte had gone to the University of Tennessee and other colleges to learn about speed. Carl noted, "Most football coaches in our area had not begun to understand the importance of teaching speed. Speed, just like strength and power, can be increased." He had become a speed guru and was teaching kids proper running technique and beginning to understand the importance of speed training on the field or track. This training translated to more wins on the football field, but it still was not as crucial as Carl's focus on being a Godly leader that invested in kids. Caledonia kids felt cared for and loved, but at the same time, challenged and accountable. Beyond that, a brotherhood was forming. A culture of putting your teammate above yourself. A culture of playing for the guy next to you. All of these things worked together to create the perfect storm of creating a football powerhouse.

The Warriors once again got banged up through the season. Their best running back, Justin Conway, was held out of the Kasson game. Kevin Klug was nursing a bad back injury, and his brother Karl had a badly sprained ankle. Both injuries were extremely painful, but both were players given the OK by the athletic trainer to play. They were not at risk of injuring themselves further; it just came down to pain tolerance. Beyond that, Coach Fruechte had decided due to their injuries, they would only play one side of the ball— that being defense. According to Carl, "defense always takes priority."

The game was a battle, and the weather was a factor. "It was like a hurricane," recalled Fruechte. Carl went on, "This limited our passing game, we liked to get the ball to our receivers Matt Frank and Jacob Hoescheit." The high-flying passing attack the Warriors used to get them to another section championship was limited. K-M was a ground and pound team, the weather was a non-factor for their offense. This gave them a distinct advantage. Caledonia missed an opportunity to score in the first half with the wind at their back. They did, however, manage to hit Matt Frank for a touchdown. The score was 7-7 at the half.

Even with the injuries and the weather, the Warriors kept it close. The game was tight, a defensive battle, in the fourth quarter, 14-7. Coach Fruechte remembers, "Karl Klug was an absolute beast that game. Even on a sprained ankle, he was a total beast." Unfortunately, the Warriors could only muster one touchdown the entire game, and Kasson-Mantorville added another late to make it 21-7. "It's my fault. Being the play-caller, I needed to find ways to score." Carl took accountability for the loss. "I remember walking off the field that game thinking we just needed to somehow create more depth."

The Kasson-Mantorville coaching staff was impressed with the Warriors. Caledonia had gained their respect. Carl reminisced, "The opposing coaches mentioned how tough Karl Klug was in that game, but I was just so proud of all the young men that year. There were a lot of tears after that game. We had great men playing for us, it was an honor to coach them. We were and still are very proud of them all." Coach Fruechte held fast to his Christian principles in losses. He would never talk poorly about a team. He would take it all on his shoulders. He was here to serve the kids; the kids were not here to serve him.

CHAPTER 9

The 2005 season had promise from the beginning. The Warriors were confident. Key returning starters were twin brothers Kevin and Karl Klug. Add to that Sophomore Zach Gran, Senior Travis Steele, and Brandon Skifton at wide receiver, and a solid line and quarterback in Cory Mesner. "We really started plugging into what Coach Hodges was doing in the weight room. That guy is amazing, he's such a dedicated hard worker, he was always willing to be there whenever he could to help us out," recalled Kevin Klug.

On top of that, Coach Fruechte had taken over the track program and encouraged all the kids to get out for track, the athletes truly started to blossom. Assisted by my old college buddy and high school track star Reese Wait, Carl began to build a track dynasty at Caledonia. Karl and Kevin Klug, Travis Steele, and Zach Gran were now four of the fastest kids in the state of Minnesota. Karl, a bit bigger in stature than his brother Kevin, started drawing the attention of Big 10 football programs. At 6-foot-3 and 215 pounds, he ran the hundred-meter dash near 11 seconds flat. Kevin was receiving Division II attention and was right there with Karl in everything. There was excitement in the little town of Caledonia for the fact that Karl was receiving some big-time recruiting attention. The community was also buzzing because the football program was coming back loaded with talent.

The fall of 2005, the Warriors started the season on fire and never looked back. They cruised to an undefeated regular season out-scoring opponents by an average of 39 to 9. It was this stretch that would bring a vision of things to come for the Caledonia program. This is the season many would point to as the beginning of the football program's dominance that very few if any, programs achieve. However, it did not come without struggle. In the middle of the season, a key player thought about quitting, Carl had to meet with him several times just to keep him on the squad. The talented athlete struggled with life at home and whether or not he wanted to stay on the team. More struggles for the Warriors would come later.

After the undefeated regular season, the Warriors of Caledonia were finally able to get past the section championship by defeating a tough Winona Cotter team at Winona State University. However, the first section championship was overshadowed by the game that followed. The matchup that everyone remembers from the 2005 season was the state-quarterfinal match-up against Minnesota Valley Lutheran. This was the first state playoff game since the 1976 state championship for Caledonia, the only championship in program history. Now, nearly 30 years later, the Warriors were hoping to replay the history of the '76 season and win it all. This could be accomplished with three straight wins. The first opponent was Minnesota Valley Lutheran, a private school in central Minnesota coached by Jim Bubholtz, with his son as QB. The game proved to be a tremendously physical battle.

Minnesota Valley Lutheran (MVL) traveled to Caledonia for the football game on an early November night. The weather was dry, yet cold and crisp. Soon after play began, the smell of freshly torn-up grass began to fill the air, along with the sound of banging shoulder pads and bodies. It was a hard-hitting game. Carl saw early in the game that MVL was keying on Karl Klug at running back and taking away Travis Steele on the outside. So, he turned to Kevin Klug and made him the workhorse. The Warriors captivated the massive crowd at Caledonia High School by scoring the game's first touchdown and taking a 7-0 lead. MVL answered back shortly after and tied the game at 7-7.

The first half ended with a 7-7 tie, a signal of things to come. MVL took the lead in the third quarter with a touchdown but failed on the extra point. They were up 13-7. The Warriors were in a position they had not been in the entire year— they were down in the second half of the game and unable to get things moving as effectively as they wanted on the offensive side of the ball. "I remember they had a couple of linebackers that were just studs, they would bring power when they hit you, it was the best team we played all year," said Karl Klug.

The fourth quarter began with the Warriors down 13-7. Coach Fruechte kept calling Kevin Klug's number. Exhausted, Kevin never backed down, not once. He kept pounding the ball. As the fourth quarter dwindled, time started to become a factor. The Warriors had a drive going, but it stalled out, and they faced a fourth and 8. Coach Fruechte dialed up Karl Klug, but not to pound the ball and break a long run like he normally did that year. This time it was a halfback pass. Karl remembers it like it was yesterday. "I rolled out after taking the handoff, and no one was open. Brandon Skifton ran a deep drag route. He was covered by a couple of guys. But, I knew it was fourth down, and we had to convert. I saw a small window open up, I threw the ball up to him, he elevated and made a great catch. Brandon did his job and did it quietly. His name may have never made the newspaper, but if he doesn't make that catch, we don't win the game."

The huge play by Skifton allowed Coach Fruechte to continue to hammer the ball on the ground with Kevin Klug. The Warriors eventually shoved the ball in the end zone but missed the extra point as the fourth quarter was coming to a close. The game was tied 13-13. MVL tried to bring the ball down the field to get the win, but it was too late—time expired. Exhausted and physically beaten, the teams faced overtime.

The Warriors lost the coin flip and had the ball first. In high school overtime, if you win the toss, it's essential to put your team on defense first. Then when you get the ball, you know if you need a touchdown, or if you can be more conservative and possibly settle for a field goal attempt. The Warriors took the field, beaten and bruised but nowhere near their breaking point. They physically hammered the ball on the ground and pushed it in the end zone. The fans went wild as the extra point sailed through the uprights, and the Warriors had a seven-point lead. The burden was now on MVL to score a touchdown, and then convert on an extra point or two-point conversion attempt.

The anticipation level was high as MVL took the ball. It didn't take long for them to match Caledonia and punch the ball in the end zone. Some of the air was taken from the Warrior's momentum, but they realized they could still win by blocking the extra point or stopping the two-point conversion. MVL decided to go for two and the win instead of attempting an extra point kick. This is the most exciting play in football. After all the hard work, advancing to the Metrodome and the semi-finals, all depended on this one play. If Caledonia stops MVL, Caledonia wins. If not, they lose a heartbreaker.

Minnesota Valley Lutheran took the field to attempt the conversion. Carl called a time-out to allow defensive coordinator Brent

Schroeder to be sure of his defensive call. The Warriors huddled on the sideline, Coach Schroeder made his call, and the Warriors were back on the field. As MVL lined up, Carl asked Brent if he was OK with the call or if he needed another time-out. No response on the headset. Carl ran to Brent, screaming, "Do you need a time out!? Do you need another time out!?" "No! We are sticking with the call!" Brent yelled back. A few quick seconds later, the ball was snapped. Bobholtz, the talented MVL QB, rolled out to his right. It was a sprint out pass to the corner of the end zone.

Sophomore Zach Gran had a feeling they were coming at him when the huddle broke before the play. "I just had a feeling," Zach said. As the ball was snapped and he saw the quarterback roll-out his direction, he knew they were coming at him. Bobholtz rolled, Zach recognized the play from film study. "When the QB rolled out, it was a predictable play after studying film all week. I saw the corner route to the back of the end zone, the QB threw it, I undercut it." Interception! Warrior fans went crazy! Zach ran the ball out of the end zone and took a hit that rolled him out of bounds. He spiked the ball and took off, running with excitement! The rest of the Warriors pulled their helmets off and showed off their bleach-blonde hair as they celebrated. The blonde hair is still a tradition every time the Warriors qualify for state. The student body stormed the field. The Warriors were headed to the dome for the state semi-finals! "I grew up a huge Vikings fan. We were about to be playing where they played. I remember thinking we are going to the Metrodome." Karl Klug recalled.

CHAPTER 10

The State Championship Run

The Warriors' first game in the Dome was dominant. They faced a talented Hawley team. However, everything seemed to be working in the Warriors favor that day. The Warriors crushed Hawley 30-14 and advanced to the first state championship game for the program in nearly three decades. Everything seemed to be going in favor of the Warriors. Now they would have a chance to prove they were the best team in the state. In one week, they'd face Eden Valley-Watkins for the right to become state champions. There was a sense of relief among a few of the team members— they made it to the championship. "Everything will take care of itself," they thought. If only it were that easy.

The week of the state championship was tense but exciting. Carl didn't worry too much about the mindset of the players. Looking back, Carl said this was a mistake. "I just thought, we made it this far, the kids will be focused. I shouldn't have to preach too much to them about staying focused." The timing was strange to have this happen, but thoughts of partying had returned to the Caledonia football program, resurfacing during the week of the biggest game in decades. "Kids were planning where to go party after the game. There was a complacency that set in that we had already arrived," reported one player. Beyond that, two players experienced trauma that week. One young man had a stabbing occur at his house. Meanwhile, the other player got kicked out of his house. Unaware of what happened, coach suspended him for part of the game after he failed to show up to practice. Stress was adding up, distractions were surfacing, but the team leaders remained confident in their ability to pull off the win.

On game day, the snow was coming down hard in Minnesota. Several inches had fallen, and travel was difficult. The Warriors left Caledonia with plenty of time to arrive at their destination. As I drove to the game, I called Carl to wish him good luck. He was in high spirits and had confidence as I talked with him. Looking back, maybe too much confidence, but everyone needs to learn that things don't take care of themselves in life. You have to fight and work to the final seconds. The Warriors were about to learn this lesson in a real way.

As the teams took the field at the Metrodome, they sized each other up. The anthem played, and the coin was flipped. In a few short hours, one of these teams would be state champs. Eden-Valley-Watkins was going to throw the first punch. They jumped to a 7-0 lead on the Warriors early in the game. The Caledonia offense stalled, unable to move the ball on a tough Eden-Valley-Watkins defense. "We just couldn't get our running game going like we wanted to," said Karl Klug. That put all the pressure on the passing game. But the passing game for Caledonia was not used to being in this type of situation. Typically, the passing game had opened up because of the dominant running game. With the running game struggling, the air attack struggled as well. Soon Eden-Valley-Watkins added another score to go up 14-0 heading into the half. "Their offensive tackle was a tough player, I couldn't do all the things I could typically do against other offensive tackles," noted Karl Klug.

Zach Gran recalls the tone at the break, "The thing I remember most is how quiet the locker room was at halftime. I wanted to say something, but I didn't feel right doing it as a sophomore. Looking back, I wish I would have stood up and said something," said Gran. With the Warriors in shock, like a boxer that just took a wicked combination of punches, they had to come back in the second half and find something that would work. Carl noticed in the halftime adjustments that their midline play should be stealing. He was frustrated with himself for not seeing it sooner.

The first play of the second half? Midline. The result? Kevin Klug ran for over 60 yards but got caught at the 5-yard line. Kevin was extremely fast; no one thought he would get caught. "Looking back, Kevin was probably extremely tired. He was our workhorse in the state tournament," Carl reflected. With Kevin getting tackled at the 5-yard line, everyone in the crowd—pretty much the entire town of Caledonia including; Brownsville, Freeburg, and Eitzen—thought a score was inevitable. It didn't happen. Eden-Valley-Watkins' tough defense put up a goal-line stand. The Warriors could not punch the ball in, and they turned it over on downs still trailing 14-0. The momentum they had just captured slipped away. Eden-Valley-Watkins took control of the ball.

Late in the third quarter, after trading possessions, Carl called the same midline play, this time to Karl Klug. Karl, a step faster and bigger than his twin brother, took it to the house with a 70-yard run. The crowd went nuts, the Warriors were on the board. As I sat in the bleachers, I thought..."it's on now." For sure, they'd roll from this point forward.

However, Eden-Valley-Watkins quickly snuffed out any dreams Caledonia had of becoming state champions by scoring again in the fourth quarter to make it 21-7. The Warriors' hopes were fading fast. They turned the ball over several times. The clock was running out. "This could not be happening. This was our year!" Those thoughts raced through everyone's mind on the Caledonia sideline as well as in the bleachers, as time slowly ticked away in the fourth quarter. The clock struck zero. Game over. Eden-Valley-Watkins became state champions with a 21-7 win over the Warriors. It was devastating.

I remember walking down on the Dome floor. A friend had given me his sideline pass so I could talk to Carl. I had no idea what I would say so I was a little nervous as I walked up to him. Carl was teared up and emotional. I had never seen him like that before. "Hey man, sorry about the loss," I said to him as I shook his hand. "It was a great season," I said. "We'll get back here Mark," he replied. I believed Carl. But it turned out, he didn't believe himself. Even though he was telling everyone Caledonia would return to the state championship, he wasn't sure he believed it. When a coach thinks of the mountains to climb to get to one state championship game, it's difficult to believe you can return. When you are exhausted at the end of the season after coming so close, it's hard to believe you have enough energy to do it again.

That December was a long one. Carl learned details about the player he had suspended for being late to practice. He couldn't believe what had happened. "Why didn't he tell me?" Carl thought to himself. Pair that with the athlete that had a stabbing at his house, Carl was mad and emotional. The cruelty of the world weighed on him. He broke down by himself in the coach's office over Christmas break. He thought, "Would we be able to get back? It was so difficult to get there, then we lost, how could this happen?" Add the emotional loss to the fact that next year's seniors had barely won a game in their freshmen and sophomore seasons, there was a reason for pessimism. However, Carl's faith and belief in the Lord served him well once again. "We are here to build boys into men that can make a positive difference in this world. We did that this year and in previous years. We will do it again." Although the emotions still ran deep, Carl rose from the ashes of the final loss in the state championship. Though it wasn't easy, like most things in life that are worthwhile, he picked himself back up and got to work. The break down was temporary.

The loss of so many talented seniors such as Karl and Kevin Klug, Travis Steele, Brandon Skifton, and Cory Mesner haunted the community of Caledonia. No one thought the next season would amount to much. This up and coming group of seniors had not experienced much success at the younger levels. The other factor that came into play was the rumor that they liked to party. As a coach at a high school, you sometimes hear rumors of certain kids or groups of kids that are into smoking or drinking. If there is hard evidence, you turn them in for a suspension. If there is no evidence, only rumors, you go and have a direct and transparent conversation with that kid. Carl heard the rumors and addressed the proper kids, but attendance at weight and speed workouts started to decline. Ernie Hodges was always ready to train the kids in the weight room, and Carl ran the speed workouts. The workouts, as always in the off-season in Minnesota, are optional. So kids can take it for granted. This particular group started to miss quite a few workouts.

It all came to a head one Saturday morning. Carl had the Saturday morning speed workout scheduled as usual, but no one showed up. Carl Fruechte is an emotional coach. He's not afraid to tell it like it is. Furthermore, when he gets mad, you need to watch yourself, you may get the wrath. The wrath will come on you like a bolt of lightning, and with good reason. It takes time for Carl to get mad about trivial things, but when it happens, it can explode. That Saturday morning would not have been a good time to have a conversation with Carl. He was upset, no doubt about it. As a result, he called a team meeting the next week. What followed was an old-fashioned butt-chewing...Carl Fruechte style. "What are we doing here?! Do we want to get better?!" Carl got up close and personal with the senior leaders, but next was junior Kody Moore, the heir apparent at quarterback. "You are supposed to be my quarterback, and this is how you are leading?!" Carl let him have it. Kody remembers it well. "Carl got in my face and let me have it. I'll never forget that. But the good thing is that it was a wake-up call for our team. We became way more dedicated after that loud meeting, and I made sure I stepped up," Kody said.

Some people may read this and think, "Man, Carl is a jerk for getting in people's faces like that." I would say the opposite. Carl is a father figure. Fathers (and parents) need to hold kids accountable. It's rare to find a coach that can get in your face, but when it happens, the kids usually wake up and change. Carl has that magic. He can give you a major butt-chewing, it might bother you for a few minutes then you realize it's because he wants you to be better. It's because Carl doesn't want you to settle for less than what you are capable of. And, Carl doesn't complain behind a closed door when you aren't performing, or making mistakes, he lets you know about it. Sometimes it's communicated in love with a serious, quiet conversation. Sometimes it's delivered—still with love—in a loud, in-your-face way. When the kids know they are loved and cared for, beyond the football field and in their personal life, you can get on their case, and they will pick up and move on, and they will respect you more for it. Carl remembers that meeting. "Everything is about timing. You can't yell all the time and expect kids to respond. That meeting was the last draw for this group. I got on them hard, and they responded," said Carl.

Workout attendance picked up after the meeting. It was a wake-up call for the kids, and they were now dialed in. Ernie Hodges was in the weight room when he could be. His way of motivating and creating discipline was beginning to gain even more momentum. If Carl and the staff could get the kids to buy in, Ernie would get them to work. The energy rolled into the summer and the initial weeks of camp. The community of Caledonia had low expectations. They looked at the players the team had lost, then looked at the lack of success the seniors had and drew a dark conclusion. Caledonia was going to slip back into average.

Carl and his staff had different plans. Carl Fruechte always sees the best in people and believes that people will work hard and maximize their abilities. It's faith, stemming from his faith in God. Faith of the unseen. Faith that kids have good in them that will win over the evil in the world. The kids just need direction and leadership. Carl, Ernie, Brent Schroeder, and the rest of the Caledonia staff would provide that leadership. Would the kids respond? Their nemesis Plainview-Elgin-Millville would be ready to test them week one.

It was a warm, humid night in September 2006, as the Warriors prepared to take the field. Kody Moore, the new varsity quarterback for Caledonia, remembers his first start well. "I was anxious and nervous. The butterflies were flying for sure." The first drive vs. PEM took those butterflies away. Kody led his team down the field immediately. He finished the drive with a touchdown pass to Simon Augedahl. "Simon was a stud. The best receiver I've ever seen. He was also a great defensive end." Recalled Moore. The Warriors extended their first-half lead to 10-0 before the break. Kody was not perfect, the future football coach admits he struggled. He threw some bad passes and interceptions, but the defense was talented. With players like Augedahl, Dustin King, and Zach Gran, they were able to shut out their rivals in the first half.

The Bulldogs came out and cut the lead to 10-6 in the second half. As always, the games against Plainview-Elgin-Millville were intense. Ever-present was the scream of Carl Fruechte on the sideline. Not a scream that is taken as a butt chewing, but a scream that says, "do it right and do it hard because I love this team." With the never-quit attitude that was developing in the Caledonia Warriors, the team was able to punch in one more touchdown. Andrell Hudson at 5 foot 8 and 220 pounds, known as "Mookie," pounded the ball in for a score making it 16-6. The defense held on, and the Warriors started the season with a huge win over their rival Plainview-Elgin-Millville.

Caledonia captured the momentum from that first game and won two more. Then Rushford-Peterson (RP) came to town. Carl and the Caledonia coaches highly respected Jim Reinhardt and the program he built. A smaller school with a great tradition, RP was talented and ready to play when they rolled into Caledonia. What followed was another epic battle in the legend of Caledonia football. It was a tight, three-overtime game that came down to one last field goal in the final overtime. Caledonia's Simon Augedahl attempted the kick, but it went high over the upright. Everyone thought it was good, but the officials signaled no good. The Warriors fell to 3-1 with a 30-27 loss to Rushford-Peterson. This would end up being the last time Caledonia ever lost a home football game.

The regular season ended at 6-2, with a loss against Chatfield. Then the Warriors moved on to the section playoffs and entered wins over Dover-Eyota and Kingsland. The team headed into the section championship 8-2 with some momentum, facing the number one team in the state, Winona Cotter. It was a rematch of the last year's section championship. Carl had a ton of respect for Pat Boland and the program he had built at Winona Cotter. That year, the Cotter team was pass-oriented. With quarterback Thomas O'Brien and receiver David Leif leading a talented group, Winona Cotter would sling the ball through the air on offense. The Warriors were ready for action and came out of the gate strong. They took a 10-7 lead into the half. But the second half was all Cotter, which thwarted the Warriors' dream of returning to the state championship. Cotter shut down the run game and connected on key passing plays to come back and win 21-10. Even though the Warriors lost, Coach Fruechte reflects on that season as one of the best coaching seasons he and his staff ever had. "Our freshman coach, Phil Costigan, did a great job with these kids when they were younger, but they didn't win a lot. The fact that we were able to go 8-3 with this group was evidence that our weight and speed programs were working. We improved their abilities with our year-round workouts. This group was a tough one to keep on task, but despite that, the system was proving to work," Fruechte said.

CHAPTER 11

"Hey Carl, not a great year for your football team, eh?" Spouted off some guy at Good Times restaurant in Caledonia. The night before, the team had lost to Winona Cotter in the section championship. Carl was in no mood to listen to this as he sat with his wife Becky for dinner. "Maybe next year can be better?" That was the last draw for Carl. He stood up and firmly addressed the man. "Hey, buddy!" Carl escalated his voice. "We go 8-3 every year, you know where I end my career? In the hall of fame." If you know Carl, this may be the only time in his life he talked about the hall of fame. It is so unusual for Carl to take any credit whatsoever. That boldness, combined with his tone, ended the conversation. Carl knew it wasn't about the wins and losses, but that's all some people can see. He knew they made a difference in the lives of those kids in 2006. Most of them still come back and visit or keep in close contact with Carl. He loved that team's effort and wasn't going to let anyone talk down on them.

Optimism was high for the Caledonia program in 2007, and for a good reason. The returning seniors and juniors were talented and hard-working kids. This group had now grown up in a culture that was exhibiting hard work, humility, and so many other exceptional qualities that every high school program envies. Senior quarterback Kody Moore returned along with talented senior, Zach Gran who played running back and cornerback.

The off-season cruised by with the players and coaches constantly focused on what they could do better. Ernie was building kids in the weight room. While there, he was always teaching life lessons and mindset to the players. Carl began investigating further methods to improve football speed. He had visited many schools, including Tennessee and the University of Iowa. He also became interested in Coach Dale Baskett, who had been writing speed articles for the magazine, *American Football Monthly*. Carl was fast becoming a speed guru. His work with Karl and Kevin Klug was high profile because they had gone on to play college football— Karl at the University of Iowa and

Kevin at Mankato State University. Coach Fruechte was obsessed with getting every single kid faster, and it was working.

That summer, the coaching staff started taking the team to the Augustana team camp in Sioux Falls, South Dakota. They had been attending a team camp for years at the University of South Dakota in Vermillion, but Carl felt a change was in order. One of Carl's core beliefs is continuously challenging his team. In the off-season, this happens in the weight room and with the speed workouts. If you attend a Warriors practice, it's intense, but not very physical. With the changing views of football and contact in practice, the Caledonia staff was ahead of the curve. In place of physical contact in practice, team camps were a great way to test your team. Carl asked the Augustana coaching staff each year to scrimmage the biggest schools. This included Sioux Falls Roosevelt, Lincoln, and Washington. These schools had enrollments over 12-15 times what Caledonia had. They may have dwarfed Caledonia, but it was here Carl remembers a quality being born in his teams. A quality that had always been there, but was refined that summer and carried over into future teams. A brotherhood was beginning to form.

At that camp, the Sioux Falls schools were bigger and stronger in many ways, but the Warriors brought a grit with them that is rarely seen in any team, anywhere in high school football. "Our team was like a bunch of bb's out there. We weren't always as big as other teams, but we were fast, and we'd hit," Carl said. Things got a little "chippy" with these big schools. The Warriors would not back down. They displayed intensity and solidified a team bond that the big schools could not match. That bond strengthed even more during an intense moment at one specific full-contact scrimmage. The big school from Sioux Falls was not having success against the smaller Caledonia school. Smaller by enrollment and stature, the Warriors frustrated their opponent. Led by fiery competitors like Cody Peterson, Dustin King, Dan Muenkel, Ryan Goetzinger, and Andy Bauer. The Warriors flew around and punished the opposition. The scrimmage finished with Caledonia having the momentum, outplaying the large city school. The team circled up for a breakdown as the scrimmage ended, and the sun had set. "We will not back down from anyone! Teams may be bigger, but we will always play with more intensity and never quit," was the war-cry of the seniors that year. That has been one of the many attributes the Warriors have carried over into every season for over a decade. It became who they are, it was no longer something they were trying to attain. Tenacious play and a no-quit attitude was solidified in the soul of every Caledonia football player. Beyond that, a real sense of brotherhood began to form— a brotherhood that would bond these players for a lifetime.

CHAPTER 12

Flying high from the confidence gained at the Augustana football camp, the Warriors were poised for success. Falling short of winning the title was not an option for this group. Despite thoughts of a state championship running through his mind, Carl continued to focus on putting his faith first and building the young men into people of character and integrity. Carl and his staff regularly preached about life lessons and what it would take to succeed in football and life. Social struggles that occurred the week before the 2005 state championship game had to be avoided. Carl and Becky continued to have kids over to visit, with a focus to pour into the lives of young men in Caledonia. Carl believed winning would take care of itself. "As coaches, we always put pressure on ourselves to win, we want to win! Jesus Christ was here to win! But he did that by investing in people. We have to keep the main thing team-oriented by getting to know every kid. We can still get on the kids and be intense, they just always need to know our coaching staff loves them, and we are here for them."

The Warriors rolled. The first seven games of the 2007 season, they outscored opponents 31-7. It was reminiscent of the 2005 season— a punishing defense and a potent offense. The first 7 games included wins over rivals Plainview-Elgin-Millville, Chatfield, and Rushford-Peterson; opponents the Warriors have always greatly respected. Week 8, the final week of the regular season, another rival was waiting. Southland High School, located in Adams, Minnesota, would be a tough opponent to finish a perfect regular season and head into the playoffs undefeated. Confidence was high as the team took the 45-minute bus trip west.

The Warriors finally arrived in Adams for the game and unloaded the bus, ready to play. The wind blew as it started to rain. Soon after the rain started falling, Ernie Hodges' son Eddie, a junior defensive end, remembers thinking, "Here we go. It's on." The rain excited the team, and they were ready to finish the season strong. Just after the opening kickoff, the game became a mud fest. White jerseys quickly turned brown, caked in mud on the torn-up Southland football field, but the Warriors didn't stop and brought the fight that was solidified in them over the year.

The game turned into a tight, back and forth battle on the wet, sloppy field. Neither team produced much offense. As the teams slipped around on the field, it was obvious this game would be a battle of defense and field position. The Warriors didn't help themselves; they were hit with a multitude of penalties and turned the ball over several times. "At halftime, we headed to the bus. Carl blew-up on us," Eddie recalled. It wasn't for lack of effort or even lack of focus. Carl blew-up because he knew the Warriors were the better team, but the penalties and turnovers would kill them if they didn't step up. Coach Fruechte fully believed in this team, and they were just underperforming and needed some kick to get going.

Hamstrung by those penalties and turnovers, the Warriors found themselves behind 14-13 late in the fourth quarter. Time was running out. Carl called a hook and ladder play to get the ball into the hands of Zach Gran. It was executed to near perfection. Kody Moore hit the receiver as Zach timed the pitch. He took it and went sprinting down the field. Zach, one of the fastest players in program history, streaked toward the end zone for the sure victory, but the muddy fields must have slowed him down just enough that the fastest Southland player could catch him on the 5-yard line. That's just what happened. Zach was stopped at the 5. The Warriors were down by one point and had time for just a few plays, none of which were successful. They had to settle for a field goal attempt for the win.

As the kicking team took the field. Everyone watched with anticipation. In the bleachers, both sets of fans hoped to end their season with an undefeated conference title. The Warriors lined up for the kick. Southland lined up for the block. As the ball left the foot of the kicker, it went up and wide right. Southland fans erupted. The Warriors and their supporters were shocked. This was going to be the perfect season, but it was now tarnished with a 7-1 record heading into the playoffs.

When a team loses a big game, many coaches walk away angry and frustrated. They say little to their team because they did not achieve their goal. Coach Fruechte wanted to win, but there was so much more to it. In the middle of a mud-soaked disappointment, Carl's relationship with his players took over. Was he mad or angry? Was this a time he would use some of his leadership capital to get on them? No. Instead, Carl walked around to as many kids as possible and told them how proud he was of them. He told them they played hard. Carl then sat down and began to ask the guys what they could learn from this night. The players gave their feedback:

"We are not invincible, that's for sure."

"We need to work hard and get better if we are going to win the state championship."

"We need to focus on execution, eliminating penalties and turnovers." Carl, who often will tell people, "I'm not very smart," was a coaching genius this night. Leading his team with integrity, showing them that winning was important, but what we learn from football is the most important thing. The kids themselves stepped up with his probing questions and proclaimed what had to be done. The kids took ownership. Zach Gran stood up and said, "What I learned from this is no one can beat us if we play our best game. Tonight wasn't our best game."

Working with people in any capacity is filled with tough dynamics; it's amplified when it's high school boys. One member of the team, or a classmate, can start rumors or a belief that starts to tear at the fabric of your program. Doubts began to creep in. "If we can't beat Southland, can we win in the playoffs? Are we good enough to win it all?" The loss of momentum with a defeat in the final regular-season game can tear teams apart. Carl and his staff learned from previous years how to head this off. They quickly addressed the doubts they knew would arise and replaced them with belief. Belief is one of the most important qualities we possess as humans. If we can see it in our minds, we are much more likely to achieve it. The Warrior staff started working on the belief of the players immediately after the Southland loss, and it paid off. The Warriors quickly refocused. They took the negative and turned it into a positive. It was a wake-up call that came at just the right time and was used for good by the right leader.

Caledonia applied the lessons from the Southland game. They rolled through the first 3 games of section play with wins over Kingsland, St. Charles, and Dover-Eyota. This qualified them for the 8-team state playoff team for the second time in three seasons. They would open their state schedule at a neutral site in Park of Cottage Grove, where they would face the Norwood-Young America Raiders. The Raiders traveled from just outside the southwest Minneapolis suburbs to face the Warriors. As the Warriors studied the film, Norwood looked huge and talented. This would be a tough test.

Norwood-Young-America was chippy. Their fans and parents were loud. All high school parents can be boisterous from time to time, but this was another level. Also, the undersized Warriors were in awe of the size of the Raiders linemen. "They looked like a college line," recalled many of the players. The Raiders came out swinging. They knew they had to contain Ryan Goetzinger, Caledonia's stud linebacker, and the explosive defensive line. The Raiders did just that and headed into halftime leading 7-0.

Carl kept it positive at halftime. There was a feeling throughout the locker room—a sense of brotherhood—the feeling that we will never quit. The feeling the team had on that summer night in Augustana began to resurface on that cold Minnesota evening. "All I know is we weren't going to roll over for these guys," said junior Eddie Hodges. "I could sense we were wearing on them, the rest of the team felt it too. We couldn't wait to get back out there after halftime."

The Warriors came out with an attitude that they would not back down. You might be bigger than us, but we're tougher, and we are about to bring everything we have. You get one of us, you get all of us, we are a brotherhood. The Warriors began to dominate the second half, tying the game 7-7 then taking a 16-13 lead. "I watched them quit. I knew by the fourth quarter we had them. There's no way we would quit, but I watched them give up," Eddie Hodges recalled. As time ran out, the Warriors held on to the 16-13 lead to win the game. They had beaten a tough Norwood-Young America team into submission. Now, there were 4 teams left.

The next opponent was another familiar face from 2005. Hawley met Caledonia in the state semi-finals. The Warriors weren't about to mess around with the Hawley Nuggets. They rolled to a 35-20 victory and headed into the state championship against the Luverne Cardinals. A great man and coach, Todd Oye, led Luverne's football team. They were back in the Prep Bowl for the second straight year. Triton humiliated them the year prior, 70-21. They were ready for the Warriors and their shot at a state championship.

The week leading up to the game was different this year. Carl refused to assume that his team would be ready just because it was the state championship. All week the coaching staff stressed the importance of the players taking care of their bodies, eating well, and preparing mentally to finish well. Kody Moore said the motto that week was, "we won't settle for second." The week of practice went well, the Warriors would be ready to go, but there was one more thing to do.

Carl pulled the kids together for one last team meeting before the Friday game. He instructed the kids to bring their parents and to be ready to talk about what football has done for their lives and why it was so important. He told the players to be prepared to share what winning a state championship would mean. The seniors stepped up in this intimate meeting. Team members shared thoughts and feelings from their hearts. What followed was an emotion-filled night that locked the team into the task at hand. "I remember getting up and talking and getting emotional," said Zach Gran. "We poured our hearts out and everything came into focus."

The next morning, the team loaded up for the three-hour bus ride to the Metrodome. Almost every business had shut down back home for the game. It seemed no one was left behind in the small town. The Warriors used the time on the big yellow bus to get locked in for the game. Like Caledonia, the Luverne Cardinals had lost only one game to Harrisburg, South Dakota, in the 2007 season. It was a close overtime game with a 23-20 final score. Luverne was hungry coming off its prep bowl loss the year prior. They had the talent to back it up. The game promised to be a tight, hard-fought contest.

The championship game had few highlights when it came to big plays. But many players who played in the 2007 Prep Bowl would say it was the most intense event ever. The Warriors got on the board first with a long drive that concluded with a short touchdown pass from Kody Moore to Andy Bauer. Soon after, Caledonia muffed a punt. The Cardinals took advantage of a short field and tied the game 7-7. The teams traded possessions and slugged it out defensively the rest of the first half. Luverne got into position just before the half to try a long field goal, but it was no good. The game went into halftime 7-7. You could cut the tension with a knife.

At halftime, there was no blow-up. Carl mentally led the young men back to the meeting they had the night before. "Play for each other. Let's send this senior class out on top. Play for the brother next to you. Sacrifice for the guy next to you." This brought the team back to its purpose. Was it about winning? Yes. It was also about doing it for your brother. Except for Zach Gran, football is as close as most of these young men would ever get to war, thank goodness. When men are in a war together, or a stressful situation like a football game, the bond they have with one another is solidified like steel. If it's done right, the other team members are more important than the individual. It was with that mindset that Caledonia took the field for the second half.

The defensive slugfest continued. It was indeed anyone's game. The Warriors put together a drive late in the third quarter and punched it deep into Cardinal territory. Butterflies flew in the stomachs of the fans and parents from Caledonia. The tension was almost unbearable for the fans as the Warriors approached the red zone. On third down inside the Cardinal twenty yard line, Carl called a swing screen to Zach Gran. Zach remembers it well. "I caught the ball, and Lee Burg threw a huge block to spring me. Everyone did their part." Zach sprinted to the end zone, the crowd exploded! Caledonia took the 14-7 lead late in the third quarter. Now, it was time for the defense to hold on for the win.

Brent Schroeder is a bold defensive game caller. He will take chances and throw unorthodox defenses in the game to confuse you. This group led by standouts Ryan Goetzinger, Mitch Meiners, Kevin Voight, Dustin King, and Dan Muenkel was not going to disappoint. They flew around, chasing down ball carriers and punishing them. "It was a great group to coach. They were so fast and had such tenacity. They were all great, coachable kids," recalled Schroeder. The Warriors held Luverne out of the end zone and the offense took possession with about six minutes left in the fourth quarter. They gave the ball to their star running back, Zach Gran, and he took the load upon his shoulders. The clock was burning down as the Warriors took the ball down the field in small bursts of yardage. But, as time was running down and the Warriors were moving the ball, they faced a fourth and 1 just into Luverne's territory. The Cardinals called a timeout. The Warriors came to the sideline, and Carl asked them what they wanted to do. Like usual, he gave the kids the ability to make a crucial decision. The players agreed, they wanted to go for the first down and seal the game. Carl approved, and they took the field. One yard and Caledonia would win its first state championship in 21 years.

Zach Gran relived the moment, "I think coach called a 442. I got the ball and I knew I had to get a yard." This is the play everyone remembers from that first state championship. Fourth and one, the ball was handed off to Gran. Luverne's Jeremy Hoff met Zach in the hole before the first down marker, but Zach pushed him backward. It was so close the officials spotted the ball and called for a measurement. Did Zach's extra effort get him the first down? The referee stretched out the chains. The nose of the ball was just past the yard marker. First down! The crowd exploded! Caledonia was just about to win the championship game! The players and coaches had the amazing feeling rush into them that they were just about to win. Roger Knutson, a long-time assistant coach, tried to congratulate Carl. Coach Fruechte said, "No, not until the clock says zero!"

The clock did wind-down to zero. The Warriors were state champions. Kody Moore vividly remembers that day. "It felt like it was a dream. There were so many fans. Carl was emotional and teared up a little bit. Dan Menkle gave Carl a huge hug. The work finally paid off...exactly 10-years after he took over the program," Moore said. Ernie Hodges rejoiced with his son Eddie and recalled the years of hard work in the weight room. The coaching staff, including Brent Schroeder, Roger Knutson, and Mitch Mullins, celebrated with fans and the players.

CHAPTER 13

Seek, and You Shall Find.

Ten years. Eleven seasons. There have been ups and downs; life and death; winning and losing. Exhaustive effort and determination; a shared vision; never quitting, these are just a few of the emotions and qualities that were required to clinch that first state championship. The city of Caledonia rejoiced. The coaching staff and players enjoyed the championship victory. Well, for a little while. To Carl Fruechte, it was quickly time to get back to work. He didn't relax for long. Carl was investigating how he could get his kids faster. His vision was to change the way small-town football was viewed. He knew to do this, he needed faster kids. Not just the top athletes. He wanted to find a way to make average kids faster. If the average kid got faster, he'd quickly become a good football player. In addition, good players would become great, and great players, elite. This would become the formula for success for Carl and the Warriors for years to come.

How could this be accomplished? Carl had researched and met with a variety of college coaches, but one person that always stood out to him was a man named Dale Baskett. Dale had been writing articles for *American Football Monthly* magazine. Carl had been studying his articles and had been very intrigued; so, he decided to reach out to him.

Dale Baskett, a straight-shooting, loquacious, hard-working, conservative man living in California labeled himself the first-speed coach in the United States. He had been teaching speed in a variety of locations for years. Coach Baskett taught high school kids, college kids, and finally worked with NFL teams and players. He had made a difference in speed development across the nation. That didn't intimidate Carl, nor did it keep him from reaching out to Coach Baskett. The communication started with emails and developed into phone calls. Then Carl hired Dale to come in and do a speed camp for the athletes at Caledonia High School. Dale came in and met with the coaching staff several times and ran several hours of speed work over two days. Carl learned, asked questions, and developed a stable relationship with Dale.

One speed camp is great; it can get kids moving in the right direction. But for programs that have a guy like Dale Baskett come in, the real work starts when he leaves. When Dale wrapped up the camp, it was up to Carl to work with the kids daily to make sure they maintained the technique and worked the proper programs to increase speed and agility. This is where Carl thrives. He began providing a variety of opportunities for kids to come in and work on their speed. If one or two kids called Carl and asked if they could do a speed workout early in the morning, Carl would always say yes. Even for one kid. A vital part of the system for a dominant football program was taking shape. The weight room was thriving, Ernie was helping kids get bigger and stronger as much as his trucking schedule allowed. Now, Carl had a clear direction and a direct line to one of the best speed coaches in the nation.

As a result of the overall system thriving, the 2008 season kicked off strong. Caledonia started the year with convincing wins over St. Charles and Dover-Eyota. Week 3, the Warriors faced rival Plainview-Elgin-Millville. In a classic game, Caledonia lost 28-25 in Plainview. The loss would prove to be the only one of the 2008 season. The Warriors rolled through the regular season and the section playoffs, entering the state tournament 10-1.

"Teams just had a hard time handling our speed," recalls Carl. This has been a problem for opposing teams in the state of Minnesota from the mid-2000s until today. It doesn't seem to be going away anytime soon. Norwood-Young America was once again the first opponent Caledonia faced in the state tournament. The Raiders were big, strong, and talented, but there was a brotherhood that had developed in Caledonia that could not seem to be broken. Pair that with the relentless, never-surrender attitude that the teams carried, and Caledonia quickly became a tough team to contend with.

The Warriors dominated Norwood-Young America 21-0. Caledonia's football program was quickly coming into greatness. The Warriors had developed an attitude that can be seen in dominant football teams across the nation but can rarely be explained. The team took the field every game expecting to win but not expecting it to be easy. The players kept their composure when things went wrong— never losing the faith that they would succeed in the end. It's almost like they believed they would win no matter what. The game can play out in a variety of ways; it may be a blowout or a close game. However, it played out, there was always a calm, confident belief that the opposing team would break at some point. Because Caledonia was so well-coached, fast, and strong, the team would seize their opponent at the right time. As Sun Tsu said, "Opportunities are multiplied as they are seized." The Warriors would seize the opportunity, grab the opponent by the proverbial throat, and never let go. At that point, they knew they had you right where they wanted you.

After the first-round win over Norwood-Young America, the Warriors rolled over Moose Lake-Willow River at the Metrodome— 44-13. The Moose Lake-Willow River Rebels would become a familiar opponent through the years. They would come close to beating the Warriors but would never quite breakthrough. Led by Dave Louzek, a man Carl greatly respects, the Rebels from Northern Minnesota would become one of those teams that could never get past the "Caledonia roadblock."

Another one of those teams, a team that played Caledonia many times and failed to beat them, was the Luverne Cardinals. The Warriors and Cardinals now faced off for the second time in the Minnesota Class 2A Prep Bowl. The year before, Caledonia won an intense game with Luverne by a score of 14-7. This year? Caledonia's combination of speed, strength, and attitude was just too much for the Cardinals. The game ended with a 47-7 blow-out. Caledonia repeated as state champions. For the seniors, living through not one but two state championships was an unbelievable feeling. After the game, a reporter tried to get Carl to talk poorly about Luverne head coach Todd Oye. Carl would have none of it and quickly shut the reporter down. One thing that is unacceptable in Carl's world is to talk poorly about a man who has coached his team to three-straight state championship game appearances. Luverne may have fallen short, but they were still champions, with great football tradition.

Carl spent the previous off-season searching for a speed program he could buy into. He found it with Dale Baskett. The other pieces of the puzzle, of course, were Ernie Hodges in the weight room and Brent

Schroeder as the defensive coordinator. Zach Hauser, soon to become a state championship football coach himself, referred to Carl, Ernie, and Brent as the three-headed monster of Caledonia football. Carl, no doubt the leader, with Ernie doing his job in the weight room and Brent coordinating a great defense year in and year out. But most of all, Carl still believed in his coaching philosophy. He believed he was building strong men, future leaders. The championships were a by-product of his investment in the kids of the Caledonia area and his faith in God.

CHAPTER 14

Three in a Row or Uncertainty?

In the summer of 2009, I invited Carl and the Warriors over to Mankato West for a mid-summer scrimmage. Carl loaded the team on a big yellow bus and traveled two and a half hours to Mankato to scrimmage our team. That summer, we were both defending state champions. Mankato West was in class 4A (the second-largest class of football at that time in Minnesota) and Caledonia in 2A, a class of smaller schools. Our team returned one of the best offensive and defensive lines we put on the field in my 11 years as head coach. Colby Straka, Jake Schoettler, Hunter Wanderscheid, Matt Sieberg, and Taylor Flanagan were tough, big, and athletic. The smallest among the group was probably 230 pounds, yet I knew what was coming on that bus. Caledonia brought a bunch of strong yet undersized linemen that would be anxious to prove 2A football is every bit as good as 4A.

I warned our players before Caledonia arrived, "They are going to be smaller than you, but they are going to be nuts. They are going to play their butts off and try to stick it to you." As the Warriors unloaded the bus and entered the locker room with us, I heard someone say, "Hey, cousin!" It was my younger cousin that I hadn't seen in years, Joey Macejik. It was cool to see him, but as I looked into the eyes of our team, I could see they were thinking, "Really, these guys don't look that tough."

What followed was a wake-up call. The Warriors defense had this yell they did— it's actually a shriek. It's a little intimidating. I believe our boys started thinking, "Coach was right about one thing, these guys are nuts." They quickly found out how fast, strong and well-trained the Warriors were for an undersized team. Brent Schroeder's defense put it on us, hard. We didn't get anything going. We had a great line and one of the best running backs in program history in Andy Pfeifer. We had future Big Ten quarterback Philip Nelson, and we also had Nick Kaus and Des Spann, two great receivers. However, we couldn't protect our quarterback, and we couldn't handle the speed and quickness to get the running game going. It was embarrassing. Even though we were about to embark on an 11-1 season, this 2A team gave us everything we could handle and more. Offensively, I'm pretty sure they could have thrown the ball to Carl's son, Isaac, and scored every play. The future NFL football player was faster than everybody. As I walked away from that scrimmage, I didn't feel good about our upcoming season. I predicted Caledonia would win three state titles in a row.

The 2009 season had high hopes of a three-peat. The Warriors did not disappoint, starting the regular season strong with an 8-0. The section tournament had the same result. Although, in a 20-12 win vs. Zumbrota-Mazeppa in the section championship, Carl felt something was off. "I started subconsciously doubting things. We had to be on them constantly. All you can do is keep talking and preaching and hope you get your message through. Unbeknownst to me, there was arrogance or pride in their actions that you don't recognize as the head coach."

Next, the Warriors traveled to take on Jon Bakken's Waterville-Elysian-Morristown's Buccaneers in the first round of the state tournament. The game was held at a neutral site in Rochester, Minnesota at Rochester Community and Technical College. The Warriors jumped out to a 7-6 lead at the half. Despite the momentum of Troy Frank's defensive score and some great catches by Isaac Fruechte, Caledonia ended up falling short 21-13. It was a devastating loss. Carl hoped to help his son Isaac and future son-in-law Troy Frank win another championship. "It's hard to change what a player's dad is telling them. Sometimes the talk at home is 'you are going to win this game,' and it seeps into the team. You can't look past teams. That's what happened with WEM," remembered Coach Fruechte.

Uncertainty

Carl Fruechte had put a lot of thought into his future with Caledonia football as head coach. He knew before the season started that 2009 was the end of the road. On the way home from the game, Carl shared with good friend Phil Costigan that he was done. Phil was flabbergasted. After the team returned to Caledonia, Carl told Brent Schroeder. Carl and Brent were walking out of the school together. Brent remembers it vividly, "Carl turned to me on the sidewalk outside

the school. He told me he was done; this was it for him. He missed
seeing his oldest daughter Alecia's volleyball games in Mankato. Carl
also told me he wanted to go watch Isaac wherever he ended up playing
college football." All Brent Schroeder could think at the
time? "Caledonia football is done."

Carl Fruechte shocked everyone with his decision to step down. Carl's
departure left doubt in a program primed for a powerful future. The
boosters and community members didn't want Carl to leave. Carl was
Caledonia football—no doubt about it. He'd worked so hard to build
the program, why would he want to leave? Carl has values. Faith and
family are the first two. Being a head high school football coach is time-
demanding. Sometimes you feel like you just can't do enough. When a
team falls short, you always question yourself and ask if you should
have or could have done more. The grind of film breakdown, practice,
youth football, and so many other commitments made it nearly
impossible for him to see his oldest daughter Alecia play college
volleyball. Now with her senior season coming up, Carl didn't want to
miss out. He also knew his son Isaac would be playing college football
somewhere on Saturdays the next fall.

All these factors didn't stop Jim Hoscheit, a key supporter of the
Caledonia football program, from attempting to get Carl to stay. Jim is a
fighter, like so many people who live in Southeastern Minnesota. But,
Jim is on another level. He lost both his arms in a farming accident
when he was young. That didn't keep him down. He contributed to his
football team in the fall of 1989 as the team's kicker. He learned how to
drive a car with prosthetics and so many other things. He went on to be
a successful businessman for Mikan companies, based in the Caledonia
community.

Jim called a meeting and hosted many of the Caledonia coaches and
supporters in his basement. They wanted Carl to stay, but he had made
up his mind that is was time to step down as the head coach. The next
question quickly became, "Who should we find to fill the position of
head coach?" Some outside names were thrown around, and all were
shut down. Someone suggested Brent Schroeder. At the meeting,
Brent deflected the idea. "What about Mitch or Roger or one of the
other assistants?" No one else was interested. It came back to Brent.
Still uneasy about taking over for Carl, he deflected the idea again.

After debating for some time, the group came to a consensus. Brent would become the head coach, but Carl would remain on staff. Josh Dierson would take the offensive play-calling duties off of Carl's plate. This would free up Carl to travel and see his kids play athletics. Brent would take over as head coach with the understanding that Carl could have the position back whenever he wanted it.

Brent Schroeder took over for Coach Fruechte as the 2010 football season approached. If Brent hadn't accepted the position, who knows where Caledonia football would be today. Brent stood in the gap those first few years. Coach Schroeder graduated the same year I did in 1995. He knew the negative behaviors kids were capable of without proper leadership. "When I was in school, the older boys would thud us against the lockers, they'd knock the books out of your hands all over the hallway floor. We would get bullied. We were the low man on the totem pole," Brent recalls. "Carl took that totem pole down, it was one group now. The seniors were now trying to help the third-grade football kids." Despite all this, Brent knew he had large shoes to fill.

The good news is that Carl never left. He was the same Carl Fruechte all year round. Carl took kids to speed camps, set up speed workouts, recruited the kids and took care of so many things. He was right there through the entire process. Brent Schroeder recalled, "Carl never left, we just flipped titles for a while." Carl had less responsibility, which freed him up to watch his college-aged kids, but he still did almost everything he had been doing in previous years when it came to program development.

During his first year in the new role, Carl intended to go watch his daughter Alecia finish her volleyball career. However, Alecia's knees were beginning to wear on her. She was struggling with knee pain. It was sometimes difficult for her to get up the stairs due to the pain. Carl needed some valuable advice from his wife, Becky. She told Carl, "Alecia needs you to tell her it's ok to have surgery and not finish her career. She's gutting this off because she knows you want to see her play." Carl choked up, called his oldest daughter, and told her it was ok not to play and encouraged her to have the surgery she needed. He was proud of her and her career.

His first year out as the head coach, Carl was in charge of the offensive line while Josh Dierson called the offensive plays. The Warriors thrived under the leadership of Carl, Brent, and Ernie and the rest of the coaching staff. An excellent lesson for the kids, it doesn't matter who gets the credit. It doesn't matter who does the interviews. What matters is the team. The Caledonia coaching staff is like a healthy marriage. They soar and struggle. They fight and makeup. In the end, they are in this thing together. It seems like it will be forever.

Brent Schroeder's career coaching record throughout six seasons was 76-3 with four state championships—unbelievable. The Warriors won the state championship Brent's first three seasons. Carl returned to call the plays in 2011 after a one-year absence. Brent took the job in 2010 when no one else wanted it, but Brent gives credit for the team's success right back to Carl and the staff. "The Vikings team of the year award we got in 2015, that's Carl's award. Carl, Ernie, and the rest of the staff," Brent Schroeder humbly remembers.

The Warriors went on to win state championships in 2010, 2011, 2012, and 2015 with Brent Schroeder as the head coach. Carl was able to watch his son Isaac play at Rochester Community and Technical College for a year, then go on to a career as a wide receiver with the Minnesota Gophers under head coach Jerry Kill. In 2015 and 2016, Isaac hooked on with the Minnesota Vikings mainly as a practice squad player but did get into some regular-season games. After two seasons, Isaac decided to let his NFL dream go. He spent time doing some speed camps before he landed with the University of Wisconsin-La Crosse and became the offensive coordinator for the Division III Eagles. He is now the wide receivers coach at the University of Northern Iowa.

Carl probably would have asked for the head coaching job back sooner, but he didn't want to cause issues with Brent. Carl could see Brent was getting stressed. He owned his own landscaping business and was finishing his master's degree. Brent was hired as a school counselor at Caledonia High School. He loves to bass fish and still runs his landscaping business. Most importantly, Brent and his wife Jenny were also raising their young family. This was taking a toll. Carl knew it. Brent knew it.

After the 2015 season, Carl sat down at breakfast with Jim and Greg Hoscheit. It came out that Carl did want the job back, but being humble he didn't say so directly. So, Greg took the initiative and said, "Carl, unless you get up on this table right now and yell you don't want the job back, I'm going to talk to Brent." Carl was silent, so Greg went to work.

Greg called Brent Schroeder and asked if they could meet up. Brent walked into the meeting and said, "Hey Greg, what's up? I thought everything went well this year. Is there something wrong?" Greg replied, "It did Brent. I just wanted to meet with you and shoot it straight. Carl wants the head job back." Brent said, "Is that it? No problem." Carl and Brent then informed Activities Director Scott Sorenson and he put his blessing on the change.

Brent knew it was time to focus on his kids, and it took some pressure off after being hired as the school counselor. Brent stated, "It's not about me, it's about Caledonia football. Carl built this program. He deserves to be the head coach. I was happy to be the high school counselor, but Carl Fruechte is the best counselor this school will ever see." Brent knew how great Carl was with the kids.

The story at the beginning of this book was from Brent's second to last year as head coach. That was the last time the Warriors lost a football game. Carl took over and continued the dominance with state championships in 2016, 2017 and 2018.

There was something built in the program through the ups and downs of the previous 23 seasons. Through the highs that came with key victories, through valleys and self-doubt that hits everyone, including Carl and his teams. A legacy was built at Caledonia High School. It went beyond football and penetrated the school culture as well as the community culture. It's possible that the disappointments of the '80s and '90s fueled the Warriors, and once they tasted the sweetness of a championship, they never wanted to let it go. But it's more than that. There are specific attributes that Caledonia has developed over time that are present in all great teams. In part two, we identify and break those attributes down. These are the attributes that so many will pursue, yet few capture them. We will look at these attributes and share stories of how they came to be instilled in a team culture.

Upper left, top to bottom: M. Hoscheit, J. Stemper, C. Smith, C. Nelson, B. Ideker, J. Colsch, J. Jannsen, C. Schroeder, C. Eglinton, J. Ross, C. King, J. St. Mary, D. Esch, M. Augedahl, M. Schoeberl, M. Moriarty, J. Chiglo, T. Meiners, J. Hauser, J. Moenck, T. Koch, J. Holzwarth, E. Storlie, J. Palen, Coach Froehling, T. Lemke, J. Rediske, K. Cavanaugh.

Caledonia Warriors from the fall of 1990. Coach Froehling front and center.

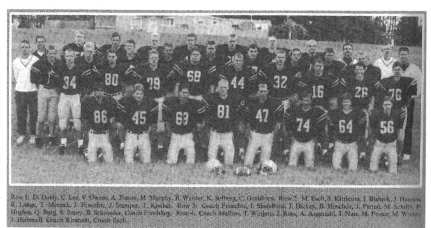

Row 1: D. Duely, C. Lee, V. Owens, A. Foster, M. Murphy, R. Weiner, K. Solberg, C. Grabhorn. Row 2: M. Esch, S. Kittleson, J. Biahnik, J. Hanson, R. Lange, T. Moenck, J. Fruechte, J. Stemper, T. Konkel. Row 3: Coach Fruechte, J. Shefelbine, J. Bickey, B. Hoscheit, J. Pelton, M. Schultz, P. Hughes, Q. Burg, S. Bauer, B. Schroeder, Coach Froehling. Row 4: Coach Mullins, T. Winjum, J. Ross, A. Augedahl, J. Nutt, M. Foster, M. Woom, J. Hammell, Coach Knutson, Coach Esch.

My senior year. I'm number 34.

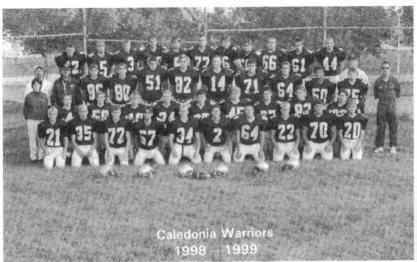

Row 4: K. Lange, Z. Hauser, P. Jilek, J.Klinski, L. King, P. Felten, J. Feine, D. Adamson, D. Bass, L. Tewes, B. Lange. 3rd row: Coach Knutson, B. Flick, T. Reining, T. Privet, J. Worsley, A. Reining, B. Scheiber, M. Diersen, B. Engen, J. Klinski, T. Hatlevig, Coach Fruechte. Row 2: Judy Techautz, K. Klug, A. Reining, D. Lange, C. Wiebke, A. Nutt, A. Schiltz, C. Klankowski, I. Schuldt, T. Denstad. Row 1: R. Jackson, J. Girard, N. Bahr, J. Paulson, C. Girard, C. Doering, F. Perez, D. Hager, J. Klug, M. Jackson.

Carl Fruechte's second year as head coach. Fall, 1998.

Carl Fruechte and John Hauser

Mark Esch and Zach Gran

Eddie and Ernie Hodges

Brent Schroeder, Ernie Hodges,

and Carl Fruechte

TRIBUTE

I was fortunate to come to know Carl while coaching his son Isaac at the collegiate level. They always say that the apple doesn't fall too far from the tree, and that personifies these two.

Carl did a great job with his family. He is a tremendous father and has taught his family the principles of life through example. He is a man of solid faith and is truly a person that puts the Lord first, his family second, and football third.

I've had the opportunity to see Carl coach his teams. His hard work is unreal. He would go anywhere he could to learn more about football and continue his progression as a coach. The best thing I can say about Carl is that his kids play for him, and is a father figure to those young men. His energy, on and off the field along with the mental and physical toughness of his teams, is a reflection of Carl. Even though he was tough, he was very compassionate for other people and would do anything for anybody. He has been tremendously loyal to Caledonia High School and the people he worked with for many years.

You will never find a more honest and loving person than Carl. I am very fortunate to know Carl, and I hope to be the man he is someday. I think his record speaks for itself, along with his championships. But I know raising those kids meant more to him than anything. That's just who he is. Enjoy the book; we will all learn a lot about life. Carl, you are an inspiration and a role model to me and many others. Thank you.

Jerry Kill
Former Head Football Coach
University of Minnesota, 2011-15

PART 2-PREFACE

Attributes that make Caledonia Football Great.

In the following pages, we are going to take a look at attributes and qualities that make Caledonia football great. It's impossible to touch on every detail that creates the Caledonia Football culture in the pages of one book. As you read this second part, take notes on what Carl and the coaching staff have done to create success on and off the field. Apply what you can to your own life or situation, and build on it.

While every person in Caledonia's program is valued and contributes to the overall success of the team, it is unavoidable that the majority of what follows will be about one man— Carl Fruechte. Without Carl, everyone would agree Caledonia would not be where it is today. He is the last to take credit for the success of the program and will deflect all praise, but that doesn't change the truth. He's genuinely a great man that is changing an entire town for generations to come. His legacy will be eternal. Carl's strong faith guides him in his mission. He's an unbelievable human being that deserves recognition. The first thing Kevin Klug, star of the 2005 team, said when I told him I was writing this book? "I'm just happy Carl Fruechte is going to get the credit he deserves.

In both parts of this book, Coach Fruechte may sound like a larger than life figure that never makes mistakes. Nothing is further from the truth. "Mark, I really screwed this up," was a statement that came out of Carl's mouth many times during the interviews for this book. Carl and the Caledonia staff make mistakes just like you and me. But the attributes we talk about in this part of the book are the type of things that help anyone overcome mistakes and keep moving forward. These lessons can apply to your team and life.

Beyond Carl, so many other people have added to the success of the program. From Brian Flick, long-time manager of the team, to Brent Schroeder, Ernie Hodges, John Hauser, Mitch Mullins, Brad King, Roger Knutson, and Josh Dierson who took over as offensive coordinator for one year. All the players who worked hard, the managers, and the community. So many have contributed. It's impossible to list them all.

Perhaps no one has sacrificed more for the program than Becky Fruechte. Behind every good man is a strong woman. Becky is that woman for Carl. She is selfless and supports Carl on every level. The longer the season extends into the playoffs, the more Carl is on edge. "I know when it is time to leave him alone. Many times the night before a game, he just needs time to himself," Becky said. Carl will drop everything to go help a player or former player, Becky has to be ready for that. It's easier now that Carl and Becky are empty nesters, but it requires support none the less. Carl recently helped a former player transfer from one college to another just before the football season started. He picked up the young man and spent hours on the road between the two schools, and even helped him move. I happened to give him a call during this time. Carl was going on just two hours of sleep. But he was determined to help.

Former players call Carl to keep in touch. Sometimes they call him before they call mom and dad. Carl has had all types of calls, more than we can talk about in one book. It's who he is as a person that makes kids want to be like him, trust him and reach out to him. Former players reach out for life advice or solely to check-in. Two young men have spent time in jail. Carl doesn't judge them; instead, he will go and visit with them and help them get their life on track.

This is one of many qualities that make Coach Fruechte and Caledonia great. It's impossible to identify every quality, but in the pages that follow, we will explore as many as possible. Many qualities work interchangeably. Not one is more important than the other. They are all needed for success.

ATTRIBUTE #1

Know Why You Are Here.

"Remember, where your treasure is, there your heart is also." Matthew 6-21 NIV

What's the most important thing happening in Caledonia? Everyone is on the same page. Why do you do what you do? If you can't answer that question immediately, you probably will never reach your full potential. Why do we want to win a state championship? Well, if Carl responded to that question, he'd tell you it's not actually about a state championship. It's about influencing young men to become the best version of themselves. Carl described Caledonia's purpose in his own words, "We talk about being a better man, someone who can contribute to the betterment of our society. We want to make better, tougher men, or ideally, better, tougher Christian men who can take care of their wives and raise great children." Winning is a by-product of focusing on the relationships and investing in kids. Let us emphasize here; the Caledonia football staff is excellent at building authentic, lasting relationships. I feel like a lot of coaches say they want relationships, but only when it gets them a specific result; that result is winning. Carl and his staff don't operate like this. They invest in all the kids in the program, from the best to the least. The coaches truly leaves no one behind. They will coach all kids the same regardless of ability. Carl stays in touch with his players, and they keep in touch with him. It's impossible to have relationships with everyone who has played and started their own lives, but Carl stays in touch with so many. "I still talk to him once a month," said Derek Adamson, one of the toughest defensive players to come through the program. Derek continued, "Carl's just the type of father figure you want your kids to be around, and you want to be around."

Carl stayed in touch with me, or maybe I stayed in touch with him. Regardless, Carl and Ernie were two of my biggest supporters, and that still rings true today. Carl would come over to La Crosse as I got older to meet up and talk. Both of them were at one of my most crucial football scrimmages when I played college football at UW-La Crosse. I could always go back to Caledonia in the summer and lift weights with Ernie or catch up with Carl. I was always welcome on the sidelines at the games. Nowadays, I don't see Ernie as much, but when I do, the bond is still there. We have a strong connection because we went through some intense workouts together. I can honestly say I wouldn't be where I am today without Ernie's influence in my life. Mostly, he never allowed me to quit. Carl, who I typically see more, ended up being a groomsman in my wedding party and one of my best friends. I'm one of many people that these guys keep tabs on. When alumni want to be part of your program years after they graduate, then you know that your football program is thriving.

So how do I jumpstart a change in my program? This may be a question you are asking. Change starts with the heart. Change begins with relationships. But for lasting change and purpose to take root, high school boys must see a glimpse of what it means to be a man. As Carl mentioned, it's "tougher men who contribute to the betterment of society." What does this mean? What does it mean to be a man? Not all will agree with what follows. The first thing that must happen is a man needs to learn how to fight. Ideally, not on the street, but a boy must learn to stand up for himself. He must learn to be tough. A boy who doesn't learn to stand up for himself is destined to a life of inadequacy until he learns to self-advocate. Hopefully, this takes place through a physical and mental struggle that team sports provide. For the physically dangerous man, which applies to most men that are drawn to football, they must learn how to control their physical power. Contact sports teach a boy to fight within controlled parameters. When they are confident in their physical ability and have positive role-modeling, they are actually less likely to become aggressive in the real world. A man who understands his physical capability for dominance but learns to control it is a good man. He who accomplishes this can be an ardent defender of what is right. He can be a protector of the weak. He can become a hero.

Additionally, a man must realize that his life is not his own. I discovered this through team sports, but most of my learning came when I had a family. Life is better when I serve others, not myself. I first experienced self-sacrifice for the good of my teammates during my senior year of football. When I learned that winning or being a part of a team was more fulfilling than reaching my personal goals, I became more comfortable in my own skin; I could be a part of something bigger than myself. As a result, not all the pressure was on me— I shared the burden with the team. It was part of the long process that helped me mature to manhood many years later.

Starting a family is the main contributing factor in becoming a man. This shifted my focus from providing for myself to meeting the needs of my wife and children. One huge problem we see in today's society is that most men fail to learn this lesson before they get married. Team sports careers revolve around themselves because mom and dad saturated him with youth sports glory. Then they either failed at the sport and fell into a downward spiral, or they excelled and didn't have the proper role models to temper their success. This can lead to pride, ego, and arrogance, and pride comes before the fall. A prideful man cannot handle hardships they have never seen or felt before. For example, when a wife must be put ahead of a husband's selfish desire, or a child who has constant needs that require a father to change a selfish lifestyle— the result? Marriages can easily dissolve, or the father becomes absent, leaving broken kids and devastated spouses. Specifically, men must learn at a young age that they are not the most important objects in the universe. They need to realize that to achieve true greatness, as Jesus Christ stated, they must be the servant of all. (Matthew 23:11)

The final and most important piece to becoming whole is accepting Jesus Christ for who He is. God in the flesh and Savior of the world. Through Him, with repentance, we are washed clean of all our sins and can stand confidently before the throne of God. For me, this was the point in life when I reached real confidence. After I accepted Christ, I was not afraid of death or failure, and I could thrive without worry or concern. At that point, I knew who I was, a child of the one True King. It amazes me that most people put more thought and research into what kind of car will buy than they do thinking about how they got on this earth. They fail to consider how they were created and came to be in existence. Before you can truly lead effectively, in my humble opinion, you need to experience the four points discussed above.

Coach Fruechte and the Caledonia football staff are teaching boys to become men. They teach young men how to fight within the rules of the great game of football and the confines of the weight room. The staff warns against the dangers of fighting on the street. They role-model and preach sacrifice— putting others before yourself. I can't think of anyone who sacrifices and serves others more than Carl. But it doesn't stop there. When selfish behavior surfaces, it is addressed swiftly and directly. Both Carl and his coaches will demand integrity and a team-first attitude. This is part of what makes them great leaders. When you have someone leading your program that will do anything for you but still holds you accountable, even in the little things like saying good morning or being polite to the custodians and lunch workers, it's absolutely contagious.

Carl also models his faith. He's not overt. He doesn't preach all day or step outside the lines when it comes to faith in a public school. But when asked, he will share. He will do so confidently and without shame. Kids observe how he lives, and they want to be like him. Faith may come a little later in life for them, but they notice, and carry it with them.

So how has positive role-modeling impacted young men in this town? Most leave Caledonia High School prepared for the journey of life; the ups and downs, the triumphs and disasters. These kids are equipped to be good people in this world and are ready to face the unknown with integrity. They are physically strong with a heart for others and are prepared to help those in need. Visualize this: your 70-year-old mother or grandmother is getting bullied by some punks in a public setting, hope, and pray that she has Caledonia football players around her. If a physically disabled kid is getting made fun of, hope and pray that kid has Caledonia football players nearby to help. If injustice is taking place, just hope and pray a Caledonia football player is on the ready. Most of these boys will do the right thing; they are strong, physically and mentally confident, and willing to act. They will stand up for what's right and stand against injustice. If we could have men like this walking around in abundance, the world would be a better place. That's what a great high school football program will produce. This is why Caledonia football is truly exceptional.

Questions:

What is Coach Fruechte's purpose statement?

Do you have a personal purpose statement? Is it something that you can quickly and clearly state when asked?

How does Caledonia build culture through relationships? How well do you create authentic, meaningful relationships with your players?

What would your players and others around your program say your purpose statement is? Would they know what you stand for?

Reflect on your purpose. Put some serious thought into it. Then come back and write it down. Share it with your team, administrators, and parents.

What types of players are you producing in your program? Do you see changes that occur because of the culture you've set up?

What stood out to you from this chapter that you could implement in your own program?

ATTRIBUTE #2

You Will Quit Before We Do. We Guarantee It. Be Relentless.

"Whatever you do, work at it with all your heart, as working for the Lord, not for human masters." Colossians 3-23 NIV

The relentless attribute didn't start on a beach in Coronado as part of SEAL training. It didn't start in a college or NFL locker room. It began in a garage across the street from the old Caledonia High School football field. It went through an old shed in Ernie Hodges' backyard, then to the stage at the former high school. It started to manifest in a weight room the Caledonia community built for kids. And now, this no-quit attitude is refined every day at the new high school in Caledonia. It has always been a part of Ernie and Carl's make-up. They are the type of people who are not going to let kids quit; they aren't going to ease up.

I was blessed to experience this firsthand at the garage, the shed, the stage, and then the community weight room. Ernie was always there for me to get in my squat workout. I remember hitting the weight room with Ernie's step-son Jesse, Mitch Schiltz, Jesse Nelson, my cousins Dustin Buttell, Chris Zaiger, and buddy Matt Woods. Eddie Hodges and Isaac Freuchte were there too. They were about 5-years-old and always hanging around us older kids. When lifting, especially squatting, Ernie would allow you to fail, but he would never let you quit. I remember one night I had to squat 410 pounds, four sets, eight reps for my college football training program.

I sat around all day, dreading the workout that was looming at the Sunday night squat session. In the late '90s, there were not a lot of kids buying into the weight room at the time, so it was a small group training. We would start around the same time, first the warm-up sets and then the work sets. We'd encourage each other during our workout, screaming and yelling at one another to push through. Football players, both college and high school, came together and worked their tails off. I remember hitting 405 pounds that first set of eight. Ernie would spot me, with a few kids on each side of the bar to help. I remember him speaking directly into my ear as I entered the squat rack. "Take the bar out strong. You can do this. It's fourth and 1, and you gotta get that first down." He'd say in his southern drawl, with intensity and focus in his voice. I wanted to get these reps for myself to get better, but equally, I didn't want to let Ernie down. I cut through the first couple of reps. I remember thinking about how heavy it was. Pushing for reps three and four were a struggle, but Ernie was there.

"Let's go! You got this! Push through! I got your back!" Ernie would say. Rep five almost exhausted me. I'm pretty sure I told him I couldn't get the last three. He said, "No-quit, dig in and drive through this. I got you! We got you." All I remember is thinking I gotta do this, and I'm not going to quit. Six, seven... I got those two reps, and I'm not sure how I just didn't want to stop. I pushed that last rep, racked the bar, and fell to the ground— totally and utterly drained. I didn't quit, I worked to the point of total exhaustion, and it made me physically and mentally tougher that day. These are the experiences Caledonia kids are regularly having now. This is a reason why they will never quit in a game. These kids will pass out on the field before they give up. It's an attitude that the weight room and Ernie Hodges will pound into you.

Carl carries himself in the same way. He's not a big weight room guy himself and leaves most of that to Ernie. That frees him up to focus on speed training. Speed is Carl's baby. In the same way, he does not allow quitting. He verbally pounds it into his players.

Most importantly, I think the players don't want to quit. They don't want to let Carl down. Just like someday, I want Jesus Christ to say, "Well done, good and faithful servant." I crave that ultimate affirmation. Likewise, the kids want the same affirmation from their head coach. The Caledonia coaches have built the relationships, the kids know the purpose behind what they are doing, and that's why they dig in and drive on when things get tough.

If you were in Caledonia in 2005, as any part of the program, you remember the first state football game the school played in since 1976. It was a state quarterfinal game, as mentioned in a previous chapter. Players and coaches alike will say this game was one of the many turning points in the program. I happened to witness the game, as well. I made the trip back to my hometown, and we were able to watch from the sideline. Some might consider it the beginning of modern-day Caledonia football. Even though that team didn't win the championship, it paved the way for future generations.

That game can be summed up as an all-out war. It was physical, hard-nosed football that went back and forth on a cold Minnesota night. The Warriors ended up winning dramatically— in overtime— and the fans quickly flooded the field. Zach Gran, who spent seven years serving as a United States Navy SEAL, remembers his teammate, senior Kevin Klug's effort. It echoed with him so profoundly the memory was etched in his mind throughout his football career at UNI and into the SEAL teams. "The one thing I remember very, very vividly about that game, was Kevin Klug. Just watching him and seeing how exhausted he was. And the fact that he just kept on playing like an absolute animal. To me, that was so inspirational going forward for the rest of my high school football career. I still remember to this day how tired he was, Carl just kept giving him the ball and he kept on pounding the rock. He was 100 percent exhausted, and he just kept on fighting."

Zach Gran was always a tough kid who never quit. But watching Kevin Klug refuse to give up impacted him greatly. It carried over into his future with Caledonia and beyond. In a hard-fought battle with Luverne for Caledonia's first championship in over 30 years, Zach's toughness showed to his teammates and coaches. Coach Schroeder remembered thinking, "that kid has an absolute heart of a warrior." Teammate Kody Moore also remembers Zach's effort in the state title game. Carl

Fruechte called him the toughest player ever to wear a Caledonia football uniform.

Gran continued, "Carl always emphasized toughness and a relentless mentality. You can't tell me guys don't carry that with them when they go out into their life and career or whatever they do. Once you start playing football in Caledonia, it's unacceptable not to be tough. It's unacceptable not to be relentless on the football field. To me, that goes a long way, and I think nowadays there is less and less of that mentality. But that's what Caledonia is all about. In the end, the willingness to be relentless, to do the work, and never quit might be a separating factor from everyone else. " Zach recalled his SEAL training as well, "I remember being in BUDS training for the SEAL program. There's no way I was going to quit. The thought of calling my family, Ernie, and Carl and telling them I quit drove me right through the training. No way was I quitting."

What is the one word that describes Coach Fruechte? One that everyone who has touched the program would agree upon? Relentless. Carl is relentless. There's no doubt, as a leader, this attitude has sunk into the entire program at all levels. Kevin Klug commented on Carl's fierce determination. "I'd run through a wall for him— because I know he would run through a wall for me. It's a combination of a lot of things, not really just one thing. Knowing how much Coach looks after each of his athletes like a father figure and truly cares about you as an athlete and a human being is the main reason why I'd run through a wall for him. It's also his coaching style. His passion for the game bleeds into his athletes and makes you want to play faster than the play before...that relentless mindset. It was the confidence he instilled in us that made playing for him so easy."

Most coaches just tell kids that they should play hard. They say, "play hard and never quit." Few coaches preach it so much that it becomes the identity of the team. Few coaches are as relentless as Carl Fruechte. But what we communicate must be followed up. This means a full effort to the finish is demanded in every drill, every rep, every practice, weight session, and game. Anything less than all-out effort is not tolerated. It will be called out and addressed, even in front of the team. It's not meant to embarrass, it's positive, it may be loud at times, but it's positive. And when the coaches develop a deep relationship with the kids instead of just knowing them on a surface level, the kids understand that they are being held accountable by the staff because their coaches truly care about them. Even assistant coaches model a relentless attitude. The coaching staff, Brent Schroeder, Ernie Hodges, and the rest of the crew, model a "no quit" attitude, I call it Caledonia stubbornness. It's been there forever. Coach Froehling alluded to it when he took the head job. Carl and his staff have simply drawn it out and used it for the good of the team.

The "finish what you start" philosophy is taken to a higher level when the kids hit the weight room. Since the day Ernie Hodges set foot in the weight room in 1996, quitting was unacceptable. The weight room plays a critical role in the development of mental toughness and an uncompromising attitude. After all, the harder you work, the harder it is to surrender. Ernie Hodges is always pushing kids to the next level. His style isn't the same as Coach Fruechte's, but effective nevertheless. He always thought you could do more weight. Just think of being in the middle of a squat workout, and Ernie quietly challenges you to add 30 pounds. But you don't believe you can do it. You tell him, "I don't know Ernie." His response? "Don't worry, I'll spot ya." And you know he will, and you know you are going to have to try. There are many times kids added a little more weight than they thought they could do. Sometimes they are successful in attempting the reps, sometimes not. But kids learn a lot when they have three to 400 pounds on their back with their buddy or Ernie behind them spotting. They learn to never quit, that's for sure.

Perhaps the most crucial aspect of implementing the no-quit attitude is the development of the will. The will to win; the will to drive on when things get tough, this is a common thread among winning teams. When it comes to being behind in a game or facing adversity, there is a way that the team responds that sends a statement. "We are ok. We got this." Nowhere was this more prevalent in the history of Caledonia football during one specific game in 2017.

It was week two. Caledonia was the two-time defending state champion, winning 29 games straight. The Warriors traveled to Dodge Center, Minnesota, to take on another rival, the Triton Cobras. The Warriors jumped out to lead 7-0, but the Cobras went on to score 27 unanswered points. Triton, led by head coach Don Henderson and quarterback Brady Essig, had the Warriors right where they wanted them. Former player Ryan Pitts was now on the sideline as a coach for the Warriors. He remembers the halftime attitude. "We were down 13-7, and for the first time since I'd been coaching, I saw the worry in the eyes of the players." Despite a bit of uncertainty, the coaches stayed calm, but more importantly, quarterback Owen King remained calm. "Owen threw some bad passes in the first half. He'd come to the sideline and take accountability, but you never saw worry in his eyes," Pitts said.

The Warriors were far from done. Pitts added, "Right after halftime they came out and scored two quick touchdowns to take that 20 point lead. Some of the young assistant coaches started saying, 'Ok, this loss will be a good learning experience for us,'" recalled Pitts. But not the veteran coaches. They'd have nothing of the sort. Carl teaches his teams how to fight. That's what had to happen. "I wasn't sure we would win, but I knew we wouldn't give up," Carl added.

Owen King, 41-0 as a starter for the Warriors, took control of the game. Owen, Carl Fruechte's nephew, son of Brad and Susan King, was raised by his parents to handle situations like this. Ryan Pitts knows the family well. "Being around the King family, I have learned so much. Brad is always teaching his family how to handle situations as they arise. He's a great father," Pitts said. Both Brad and Susan (Carl's sister) were stand-out athletes in their earlier days for Caledonia. Their athletic ability and champion mindset have clearly been passed down to their children.

Under Owen's calm leadership and strong arm, the Warriors began to dismantle the Cobras defense. "It wasn't big plays. It was systematically moving the ball down the field, then playing great defense," recalled Pitts. Down 27-7, with seven minutes left in the third quarter, Sam Barthell had a great kickoff return to set up a touchdown pass from King to Andrew Goergen to narrow the lead to 27-13. Triton drove to the Warriors 39-yard line and missed a field goal. Heading into the fourth quarter still down two scores, the Warriors went on a 91-yard drive as King hit Goergen again for the touchdown. When the Warriors cut it to one score, the Triton sideline grew quiet. The Warriors smelled blood in the water. They held Triton to a three and out, then King hit Marten Morem for another touchdown to tie the game at 27-27.

Triton fumbled on the next drive, but King gave it back to the Cobras with an interception. The two teams traded punts, but Caledonia's punt nailed the Cobras deep on their 5-yard line as time started to run out. It looked as though the game would head into overtime, but Caledonia's defense came through. They forced a fumble on Triton's 15-yard line with 1:41 to play. On a third and goal from the 13-yard line, King hit Goergen once again for the touchdown with 50 seconds left. The Cobras tried to tie, but Jordan Berg intercepted a pass to seal the deal for the Warriors. They never gave up. The will to win came through once again.

Why and how do teams solidify this so-called "will?" Will develops when everyone on the team is on the same page and has a common goal. As we learned in the previous chapter, being on the same page is a considerable part of the Caledonia football program. Once everyone has one vision, then will is simply forged like steel through hard work, sweat, and adversity. Yes, adversity—adversity tests the will. In life, having a lousy boss tests your will to do your best in the workplace. Or, think of the soldiers that have in brutal prison camps, this tests their will to live. Experiencing adversity of all types in a football program will solidify the will of the team. Many coaches, when challenges arise, put their tail between their legs, or they act like someone died. They blame the kids, the coaches, and themselves. But they don't lead. Navigating adversity is your job as a leader. Embrace tough times. Have a positive attitude and be upbeat with the players. Take the high road through adversity. As a leader, you can take two approaches: You can take the high road and meet difficulty with strength while sending the message, "we can do this," or you can lead your team down the path of negativity and despair. This road will doom your team. Perhaps the only thing worse is doing nothing. But doing nothing is not leadership, it's weakness. Doing nothing or not addressing adversity will allow negativity to fill the cracks that positive leadership should fill by its very nature.

Questions:

Be honest. Do you have a no-quit attitude? Do you push through when things get hard, or do you start to complain and blame?

From the reading above, what behaviors do the Caledonia Warriors demonstrate that creates a relentless, "finish what you start" attitude?

Does your team exhibit a no-quit attitude? If they don't, you may not be modeling it for them. You may not have built the relationships or clearly defined the purpose of your program. When you have a relationship and clear purpose, the team will develop the will necessary to drive on when things get tough. What part of this do you need to work on?

When was the last game you came from behind to win? How did that make you feel? Tell stories to your team of you or someone else being down and out, and how to comeback. Sharing stories about yourself and others is a great way to instill this attitude in your players.

ATTRIBUTE #3

Do Hard Things. Get Uncomfortable. Be Uncommon.

"That is why, for Christ's sake, I delight in weaknesses, in insults, in hardships, in persecutions, in difficulties. For when I am weak, then I am strong." 2 Corinthians 12:10 NIV

Comfort—our society today is stuck in comfort. We want to get to our nice, warm houses and sit in our comfy couches while we dial up the latest and greatest series on our T.V. We substitute interpersonal relationships for a screen. We allow the screen to raise our children so we can have a drink and relax after a hard day. We wake up and do the same thing the next day. It's repetitive. Work, home, dinner, take care of the kids, relax on the couch, and watch the screen. It's a repetitive cycle of comfort. Sometimes the kids are an annoyance, and we don't want to deal with them, so we allow them to use a screen for entertainment. And that work thing, that's where we just get by. But then the work thing eventually becomes comfortable, too. As a result, we would never consider a change. That is out of our comfort zone. After all, I need this job to pay my bills: cell phone, cable, Amazon, Netflix, Hulu, insurance, internet (we need the fastest), our overpriced car and our house that is too big and too nice. Plus, other toys.

Our kids eventually get old enough to play youth sports. We buy into the lie that they have to be doing something organized all the time. Pay-to-play sports replace backyard pick-up games. Coaches tell us our kid is really good, so we pour more money into youth sports, which, in and of themselves, are fine— for the most part. But then we do what Americans do best— we super-size our kids' schedule, just like our value meals. In doing this, we create a child-centered home instead of a parent-centered home. The child's calendar dictates the flow of our family with activities every weekend. We watch our kids and tell them how good they are, then rush home to get on the couch so we can have a drink and watch the screen to unwind. Playing in the yard with other kids is uncommon. We think youth sports are necessary to maximize their talent, even when they are 6-years-old. We've bought into the lie. As a result, we are now too busy and exhausted to do anything that stretches that comfort zone. We also think maximizing our kids' schedules somehow constitutes as relationship-building and earns us a good parenting award.

We fail to achieve our full potential because we get caught in the trap. It's easy to fall into the trap in our society. I've been there. Fortunately, many people are starting to recognize our comfort for what it is. Comfort is the thief that steals our promise. We worry about someone breaking into our house and stealing our stuff, or worse, someone taking one of our kids. I agree these things would be a nightmare, but how many times do you think that the routine you are in is stealing your potential and keeping you from doing what you are destined to do? Comfort is the enemy of progress in our lives and for our teams.

It's easy to do the easy things. It's the hard things that intimidate us. It's the thought of doing hard things that keep us on the couch. We believe hard situations would be too stressful for us, we're too busy, but we count ourselves as "busy" because we waste too much time on screens. What would happen if we challenged ourselves to do the difficult tasks, and attack the things that make us uncomfortable? You always wanted to try a different profession, write a book, take up a fitness class, or learn how to play an instrument. You have always wanted to run a business, be a public speaker, or even just be a better parent. But it's hard to read that book on parenting. It's hard to look into starting a small business on the side. It takes stepping out into the possibility of criticism and shame to do all the things you really want to do. So I'll just stay in my routine, complain about my job, and die just about average. There is nothing inherently wrong with being average; it's just that we are leaving opportunities on the table that we could pick up and pursue with greatness. But our desire to be comfortable is just too overwhelming.

Sound familiar? Even just a little bit? That's because comfort is not meant to be a permanent destination nor a lifestyle. Comfort is for after the work is done. And I'm not talking about just finishing your day at work. I'm talking about the work that pushes you to the next level. Almost everyone does the work that is necessary to get by, but few people do the work that is necessary to thrive. I want to emphasize here, "thrive" does not mean that this extra work makes you rich or famous; it's the work that can add meaning to your life that you never thought existed. But to achieve high-level purpose in your life, you must take up a more significant burden of responsibility than you had previously. This means having the difficult conversation, attacking a problem, taking on a challenge, or just stepping out in faith. It may mean starting that side business, reading or writing the book, volunteering at church, or improving your fitness level by taking a workout or martial arts class you've always wanted to take. All of these are burdens of responsibility that can help push yourself to the next level.

I'm not opposed to comfort from time-to-time. I enjoy a good movie and a glass of wine on occasion. But I can't fully appreciate it if I have something I need to do or something I should do. And, when you start looking around for things we *could do,* that's when things really start to change. "Look for work." That's the motto at our house. You should still set aside times to enjoy comfort after it is earned. Spend some time building up your hopes and dreams each day by setting goals, making a to-do list, or getting in a workout. Be productive every day, and remember to set aside time for yourself and your family. Always remember your life in order of priority: Faith, family, and then the other stuff. The priority list is not T.V., drinks, family. Reward yourself after you have five productive days, shut-off the phone, and watch a little T.V. on Friday and Saturday nights. Then spend all day on Sunday with your family and relax. But be ready to get out of your comfort zone again as Sunday night approaches.

I'm not sure if Carl Fruechte enjoys living a life of worldly comfort. His house doesn't have air conditioning, he has a flip phone instead of a smartphone, and he reads books instead of watching T.V. I know he enjoys relaxation from time to time. For example: going to Brownsville for pizza on a Saturday night, hanging out with peers at a coaching clinic, or staying a few nights in New Ulm or Stillwater biking with Becky. Carl does relax, but it's at the right time. Because Carl operates outside his comfort zone, he creates a situation where those around him— especially his players—tend to follow suit. No one will exhaust or outwork Carl. It isn't going to happen because he has limited distractions and prioritizes his life accordingly: Faith, family, and football. These beliefs keep him moving forward consistently, and when someone pushes forward every single day, they look up a year or two later and find out they have accomplished a lot more than they thought they could.

It's not easy to open the weight room three times a day in the summer so kids can make it in no matter what their job or schedule looks like — rounding kids up in a van to take them to speed camps. That's not comfortable. Having difficult conversations is not comfortable. Even just taking the time to get a kid a football, like he did with Zach Gran in second grade. Most people don't even think of it. Many coaches wouldn't stop to talk to a second-grader. Gran recalls that day because it added value to his life.

Karl Klug vividly remembers when Coach Fruechte stepped out of his comfort zone to coach him up at the Iowa football camp. "Coach came up to me and said, 'Karl, they are going to line up all the campers shortly and run some sprints, run like your life depends on it.'" Karl took his coach's advice, and after just a few sprints, the Hawkeye staff pulled him aside. He ran so well the coaches took an immediate interest and wanted to talk with him one-on-one about attending the University of

Iowa. What does this have to do with stepping out of your comfort zone? Well, most high school head football coaches are not at these camps with their players, Carl Fruechte takes the time and *goes with* his players to as many camps as he can. That's stepping out of a comfort zone, but he takes it up another level. He is giving these kids advice and teaching them the mental and emotional part of the game while the camp coaches are teaching the kids skills.

You see, God blesses us with gifts and talents. The enemy of our soul and our human nature pushes us toward comfort. If a person is blessed with large amounts of money, I believe they should use the abundance to bless others. If a rich person doesn't use their financial blessing to serve others, we call it greed. The Bible says there is an increased expectation from those who have been given much (Luke 12:48). However, I feel our Christian culture sometimes fails to see the blessing of any gift also requires us to use that gift to help others. Do you have the ability to relate to others? Failure to use that gift would be a sin, both literally and figuratively. Do you have the gift of encouragement? Then that gift is meant to be used to serve others, and if we sit back and do not use that gift, we are also guilty of greed. We are expected to use whatever talent God has given us. Carl Fruechte uses his skills to role-model for young men, encouraging them to become more. It's not always easy for him, but we can learn from him. Our giftings are not meant to make us rich financially; they are intended to make us rich spiritually. This means we need to use our gifts and dodge the gradual slide towards comfort, laziness, sloth, and indifference. We need to take action.

Questions:

Do you challenge yourself by doing hard things in life? Or do you shy away from difficulty?

Are you a person of comfort? Is there more you could do to improve yourself or your team?

What comforts could you remove from your life? What challenges can you add-in?

Are you moving forward towards your goals at a consistent pace every single day?

What stories can you share with your team about yourself or other people stepping out of their comfort zone to create a challenge in their life?

ATTRIBUTE #4

Humility, Sacrifice, and Service

"Humility is the fear of the Lord; its wages are riches and honor and life." Proverbs 22:4 NIV

If we put ourselves at the center of our own world, we become either narcissistic or depressed. When we make ourselves the center of the universe, it's all about what we can do for ourselves. As a result, we either provide abundantly for ourselves, or we end up not producing enough. If we provide generously for ourselves (big house, fancy cars, the best of everything), arrogance sneaks in. Wanting more becomes a way of life, we are never satisfied. We can become indulged in ourselves—looking around and seeing how good the world is that we built. We become our own god.

On the other hand, if we don't provide enough material goods for ourselves, we feel like failures. We might blame the world and other people for our lack of production. It's easy to become bitter and blame others. Grumbling about the way we think things should be becomes a way of life. We may slip into a state of contentment and stop pursuing true greatness. We may be afraid to take risks because of the fear of exposing ourselves as actual failures. As a result, we don't risk hurting our reputation, and if we don't risk, we don't grow.

How do we pursue true greatness? We take the focus off ourselves and put it on someone else. A key point is *someone* else, not *something* else. When we focus on serving others, their needs become more important than ours. Ideally, we help people that will never be able to repay us, so there is never an expectation of return. The way a person treats someone who can do nothing in return for them is the real test of the heart. Do you, as a leader, serve others? "I'm not a leader," you say? Yes, you are! Whether you are a parent leading your kids; a brother or sister leading your siblings; a secretary leading people in the office; a CEO, teacher, coach, or any other profession or position—you are a leader. Whether you like it or not, someone is watching you and looking to you. It may just be a few people right now; it may be a large number of people. Leadership may come in a burst of a few minutes a day, or it might be constant leadership throughout your day. But people come in and out of our lives all the time that need your guidance. Failing to see this is a failure to understand your purpose in life.

When I was in high school, it was mostly a "look out for number one" attitude. Our culture was self-centered. This started to change when the team became more significant than the individual. We began to put the needs of our team and teammates above our own needs. Looking out for yourself leads to the pursuit of self pleasures: alcohol, drugs, dominance over another person, screen addiction, and so many other vices. When we look out for only ourselves, it's almost like making ourselves a god. We may not get to the point where we go to church on Sunday and worship *ourselves*, but it becomes an I want, I need attitude. Me, me, me... It's all about me. This attitude leads to emptiness, fear, despair, and depression. The thing about a "me first" approach is that all of us are afflicted by it at some level, but even worse, we can be stricken with a "me first" approach that is destroying us, and we have no idea we have the disease. It's covert, mostly undetectable by the person who is afflicted.

When we think about only ourselves, we become selfish. The "I syndrome" sets in, then we are in trouble. We need to be constantly aware of our own selfishness, or it will destroy us. "Produce fruit in keeping with repentance." (Matthew 3:8). This is excellent advice that was given to us by John the Baptist. God spoke these words through him because God knows that repentance is the ultimate form of humility. If we genuinely admit our mistakes, we stay humble, and that takes the focus off ourselves. If we take the spotlight off ourselves, we produce fruit. We produce fruit by meekly serving others.

Here in America, we are all among the wealthiest in the world. Even our lower class is among the most affluent group in the world. On the flip side, so many people in other countries like India or continents like Africa are in real poverty. It seems to me that our wealth in America could help end so many issues, such as poverty, on a global scale. Why can't we do this? Selfishness. We "need" more. That Starbucks every morning is more valuable to us than helping someone out. That brand new vehicle... we "need" it. Can you imagine what would happen if you started investing in one other person? After we invest in one person, we add another, then another. Now we are investing in three other people. It may be sponsoring a child in a struggling country or just being a mentor to our neighbor. Do you know what would happen? I'll tell you what would happen. You'll start to win. You may not get rich, but you will begin to see change happen in the world. Why doesn't someone help me out? Well, it starts with you. No one helped you, so you are going to sit back and do nothing to help another? That is not mature; it's the meaning of selfishness. That's like a little kid saying he hit his brother because he got hit first. We don't accept that answer from kids, why do we allow it from ourselves?

Maybe you are older now—advanced in years. Imagine there's a family you know with three or four young kids and little money. You offer to watch their kids for free while mom and dad take a few hours to spend some time together. You may save their marriage and never know it. Maybe you know someone who is struggling financially while you are thriving. So, you send them a check for $500 or pay their mortgage. This actually happened to my wife and me shortly after we married, then again later in life. Those people made a real difference in our lives. We will never forget what it felt like, and we will pay that act of kindness forward someday.

Sacrifice. Another Form of Humility.

Sacrifice. It was and continues to be modeled by all the coaches in the Caledonia football program. But NFL veteran Karl Klug specifically remembered how Ernie Hodges sacrificed for the team. Ernie tirelessly worked with the athletes in the weight room. "Looking back, I didn't appreciate him as well as I should have. He came straight from his truck driving shift. He was exhausted. I could tell he was tired. But he was diligent and detailed to get you to learn the proper technique. That was huge for me so I could get to the Iowa Hawkeye program and hit the ground running," said Klug.

Even though he was dead tired, Ernie did faithfully come to the school straight from his job. Most people are not willing to sacrifice to this level. Ernie never complained of being exhausted. And to this day, he doesn't cut corners because he is not feeling well. He doesn't accept excuses. Kids can see this, and they understand the sacrifice— even if they don't know it at the time. Subconsciously, the athletes at Caledonia see sacrifice and duplicate it. If Ernie can come in and train when he is tired, nothing will stop the Warriors on the field or in the weight room. This is the attitude that has been transferred to the athletes in the Caledonia weight room.

Service and sacrifice can be as simple as how you treat others. Ernie will say "good morning" to a player as they walk in the weight room, and if the athlete doesn't return the greeting, he will address it directly and firmly— "It's common courtesy, someone says good morning, you say it back. Kids need to be taught this stuff," Ernie said. Carl and Ernie teach kids about how others should be treated. But no one models this better than Coach Freuchte. In a personal conversation, he's always polite and courteous. Carl will never miss a chance to say please and thank you. If you are walking down the hallway with him at Caledonia High School and he sees a piece of trash on the floor, he will go grab it and get it in the garbage or recycling bin. By consistently treating others with respect and doing the little things, Carl is teaching service and sacrifice. We are serving a fundamental human need of helping others feel valued when acting courteous and respectful. When people feel valued, they will run through a wall for you. Good manners and kindness are foundational concepts of service. "Kids today seem to have lower self-esteem than ever; we will do whatever we can do to build them up. Sometimes they need some direct truth as well, and we will give it to them. Kids appreciate it in the end," stated Carl.

Kevin Klug believes Coach Fruechte's servant leadership is the most critical part of why Caledonia football has thrived. "Carl's door was always open. Yes, he wanted us to get better at football, but I actually think he wanted us to be a better human being every single day. I think that it was more important to him because he knew if we became better human beings, everything else was going to take care of itself. But literally, he would do anything," Klug said. Anything even includes asking kids what they had for breakfast. If they were eating pop tarts, he'd invite them over for a more hearty meal at his house. It means if kids can't pay for a camp, he finds a way for them to go anyway. Here is one of the most common stories about Carl that dates back to my days at Caledonia. He would find speed camps and football clinics, help the kids get signed up for them, and then drive them in the school van. Zach Hauser fondly remembers those trips. "Carl would make them fun, he'd be rocking out to classic rock and playing the drums on the steering wheel," said Hauser. Ernie Hodges and assistant Mitch Mullins were never far behind, making all the trips that they could.

The Warrior football program highly values service to teammates, the youth program, and the community. Caledonia players are expected to give back. Kevin Klug remembers that Carl would say, "be great in the community." Klug continued, "We always looked forward to going to help the kids on Saturdays." The youth program was new, something Carl started early in his tenure. "I remember going to a youth camp and sometimes having five kids," Coach Fruechte recalled. "But you keep working hard and have faith that it will grow."

Great teams with servant hearts help their fellow teammates. The starting quarterback helps his backup; meanwhile, the older defensive players assist younger kids in understanding a scheme, or simply the older kids show the young kids little details that they may have missed while the coach was instructing. This willingness to help each other is a cornerstone of a dominant program. It's a "pay it forward" mentality that will be modeled by each class. It maximizes learning because if something is missed while a coach teaches a skill or scheme, a player is totally comfortable telling a teammate they need help, and the teammate is willing to help. I've experienced this first-hand when I started to learn jiu-jitsu. A couple of years ago, I joined a great gym in Edina, Minnesota. The instructors at Alliance Jiu-Jitsu, Damian Hirtz and Tim Blackstone, are fantastic people and excellent teachers. When we get out and practice on the mats, it seems all the members, especially black belts Pat Worley or George Faber willingness to help me has been critical in my development. I learn as much, if not more, from my classmates than the main instruction. When it comes to jiu-jitsu, I may actually beat them someday (years from now) with what they've taught me. In football, that younger player may beat out the person who is helping them. That's selflessness. That's sacrifice. That's a team.

Everyone on the team contributes. Even the practice squad player has something extra to give. Once again, if we measured success by high achievement, most of us would be deemed failures. Coach Fruechte serves his athletes by always seeing the best in them, no matter what role they play. Just ask his son, Isaac, "I almost think it's his greatest strength and his greatest weakness." Isaac Fruechte said about his dad. "Carl just never gives up on kids; he always sees the best in them. But when they fail or stray from the path, he takes it hard." Yes, Isaac calls his dad "Carl" on occasion, but so do many of the players. That's how

Carl started—he was never Coach Fruechte to me—he was always Carl. He never demanded anyone call him coach. He's humble.

Perhaps the most extraordinary impact of the football program at Caledonia over the years has been the influence on the other activities and the overall culture of the school itself. This book started with stories of alcohol, drugs, hazing, and fighting. Has that been eliminated? No, it never will be, but dramatic changes have occurred over the past 25 years. The school now ranks in the top 20 academically in the state. Other sports have won championships, and the weight room can barely fit the athletes that want to work out and get better. There are always a few stragglers that may still use alcohol and drugs, but overall, it is squeaky clean compared to where it was.

Humility and service are foundational pieces that every football team has to be built upon. But this also applies to your place of business and your family. Humility allows us to be honest and overcome the fear and complacency that holds us back. In the Caledonia football program, humility is a way of life. If you ask players what one of the top phrases you hear come out of Carl Fruechte's mouth, they will say, "be humble." Carl is continually saying "be humble" and teaching humility, even before the championships started. It's been a staple of his belief system long before he became a head coach. Did Caledonia really need humility when Carl first started, and the program was struggling in 1997? Did the program need humility in the middle of its 60-plus game winning streak? The answer is obvious; humility is always needed.

Questions:
From the reading, what are some ways the Caledonia staff models and teaches humility, sacrifice, and service?

Are you humble when you win? Are you teaching your team humility by sharing stories and giving examples of what humility looks like?

Make a list of how you can create humility in your team by sharing stories about yourself or others.

The best way to create humility is to serve others. What can you and your team do to reach out and help others?

How can teammates serve each other? Share this with your team or have them come up with these ideas.

ATTRIBUTE #5

Dream big. Believe Caledonia Kids can Accomplish Great Things. Fight Through Adversity.

"For I know the plans I have for you," declares the Lord, "plans to prosper you and not to harm you, plans to give you hope and a future." Jeremiah 29-11

"This could be you," Coach Fruechte said to Karl Klug. Karl was ready to head to the University of Iowa to play college ball for the Hawkeyes. Karl looked over at the newspaper Coach Fruechte had just slammed down on the table in front of him. "Karl, work hard, stay humble, and don't quit. This could be you." It was an article about Chad Greenway, the former Minnesota Vikings star linebacker who had played at the University of Iowa and made millions in the NFL. Greenway was a small-town kid from South Dakota. It was such a small town that they played 9-man football.

A few months before this conversation with his coach, Karl Klug and his twin brother Kevin went to visit a community college in Albert Lea, Minnesota, with plans to become electricians. It was a profession they would have chosen if their current endeavors failed. Like many people in Caledonia, they would choose a trade, work hard, and build a nice life. Small town life has its rewards. Speaking from experience, working hard with your hands, completing a project, or doing physical labor is rewarding. It's hard, but it's worthwhile. You feel a sense of accomplishment at the end of the day. Many times you are physically exhausted, and that actually feels great. That's the way many people in Caledonia earn a living.

Neither Karl nor Kevin really thought much about going to a 4-year college to further their education. It didn't seem like something they could do; it certainly wasn't anything their family had done before. Carl's belief fueled the Klug twins. They took Coach's advice and decided to dream big. It led to incredible success. Karl had a successful career with the Hawkeyes before being drafted in the fifth round by the Tennessee Titans. He played in the NFL for eight seasons with Tennessee. His brother, Kevin, played Division II football for Minnesota State University, Mankato. Most recently, Kevin moved to Nashville and started a business, *Klug Fitness*.

How does Carl Fruechte, a man who has never really left Caledonia, have a vision for his athletes to think big? To answer that question, we must examine his upbringing. Carl's dad Al was a significant influence in his life. From his belief system to his outlook on life, his father had an enormous impact. When Al was killed in a car accident in December 2018, it was devastating for Carl and his family. Carl is the oldest of 12 children, and he's the leader—the one they look up to for advice. He was also the closest to his dad. Carl and his father would have in-depth conversations of faith, politics, the way the world was heading, and about so much more. It was his father, however, that put dreams into Carl. He taught him to think big. Al would say, "Minnesota kids are just as talented as any other kids in this country. The Lord created everyone equal, so if you work hard, you can accomplish a lot and be as successful as anyone."

Perhaps what drives Carl most, is he didn't personally take advantage of a "think big" mindset while in high school or college. "When I played in the '80s, the coaches in Caledonia told us we'd never amount to anything." Carl remembers thinking, "there has to be a better way." After high school, he attended Winona State and tried to play college football but quickly returned home, where he has spent the rest of his life. College was overwhelming; Carl was a small-town man, and that small-town life drew him back to Caledonia. Carl admits he missed out on what could have been at Winona State. Is that a bad thing? No, not necessarily.

Sometimes God uses our disappointments in life to drive us, or better yet to help us inspire others. Does Carl wish that he gave college football a better chance? Probably. Does he use this regret to push his players to the next level? Absolutely. It's odd, but Carl's post-high school experience was turned around and used to motivate so many of the kids he coached. Furthermore, he teaches them to dream big, not letting opportunity slip through their grasp. What started as regret for Carl, has turned into a blessing for Caledonia High School. "You intended to harm me, but God intended it for good to accomplish what is now being done, the saving of many." (Genesis 50:20, NIV)

Ernie Hodges also thinks big. Most likely for the same reasons. Regret. Life is built in such a way that just a few critical decisions can lead to disappointment. For Ernie, that decision is failing to maximize his talent as a football player or not having the most cutting edge training and teaching as a player. If we have the right attitude and humble ourselves, we can share our mistakes and setbacks with those we lead, and hopefully, paint a picture of a better life for them. We can create belief using our own regrets. This confidence has spilled over to so many people in Caledonia. It has led to 10 championships and counting. It has led kids to go out, grab the world by the horns, and win. Zach Hauser took this thought process and used it to become a two-time state championship football coach. I used it to become a two-time state championship football coach, as well. Jesse Nelson used it to become a Divison I wrestler and career SEAL. Did other people help us along the way? Absolutely. I had a supportive family. My mom, dad, and brother always loved me and believed in me. But the extra edge? This attitude was taken to a new level just by being around Carl and Ernie.

What we see from Carl and Ernie is the ultimate growth mindset. The belief that we can use our God-given abilities to make a difference. We can choose to see positive in every situation. Once again, this is a Biblical principle. "Finally, brothers, whatever is true, whatever is honorable, whatever is lovely, whatever is commendable, if there is any excellence, if there is anything worthy of praise, think about these things." Philippians 4:8 ESV.

Possibly the most crucial theme in this book—one that cannot be overlooked and must be restated—is that a growth mindset and a positive outlook are valuable *everywhere* in life. And not just for successful coaches and business leaders. Remember, dreaming big and thinking positive may not lead to millions or your 15 minutes of fame. But it may lead you to your purpose, and it may help you hit the bullseye in life. Where in life would an optimistic outlook not be beneficial? Your marriage may seem bleak, but think positive—think restoration. What about a cancer diagnosis? A negative response won't help the situation. Believe in miracles. The worst thing that can happen is the miracle doesn't come. You are always in a better place with positivity. Hope is the greatest of things, never lose hope.

My buddy, Ken Essay, is living out his purpose as an elementary school principal. When I started working at Mankato West High School, he was a physical education teacher and a hockey coach. He then became an activities director, and later, an assistant principal at a middle school in the Mankato area. In all of these positions, he stayed positive, and that made a difference. It took years before he hit his sweet spot as an elementary school principal. Ken found a way to use his skills and strengths to pour into a school of teachers, students, custodians, and support staff. He's not rich, but if offered a million dollars to take a new job, he probably wouldn't accept it. His perseverance and positivity led to his purpose, and to him, that's more valuable than gold.

So, what's the point of my friend's story? Aim high. Never lose hope. See the best in people. Believe there is something great out there for you. It could be a 60-plus game winning streak as a football coach, but it may be something totally different, quite possibly not even on your radar yet. Maybe your 60-years-old, and you are still waiting. Dream big. If you still have breath, your purpose is still waiting for you. Always keep looking. Hope is what we can never afford to lose. Shoot for the stars; pursue great things; find your purpose. The only way to do it is to believe.

Be the One Who Can See Opportunity.

Today, coaches face adversity at an unprecedented level. In Minnesota, they do it for an average of $5,000 a year. To say coaches are overworked and underpaid is an understatement. Parent predicaments, year-round weight room, watching endless amounts of film, battling club sports to get kids out, and once again— parents. It has become a tireless profession that pays well below minimum wage and opens a coach up to personal scrutiny that can affect self-esteem, their family, and overall life. The only coaches that can hang on are those that honestly love the game.

However, we have to view adversity as a positive. It builds character, and it should be faced head-on. When we approach adversity with toughness and optimism, it lays the groundwork for the kids we role-model to follow suit. The philosophies that follow are a combination of ideas that worked for me as well as Caledonia football.

Let's make one thing clear: Coach Fruechte has faced all types of challenges and still does. People may think Caledonia has it on cruise control. I had a long talk with Carl not long ago after Caledonia's 62nd consecutive win. He shared with me how there were some serious issues on the team that needed to be dealt with. It led to a kid coming into his office in tears, but it had to be addressed. You see, it's how we react to adversity that reflects our real character. Remember, Caledonia has a great thing going, but sitting with Carl and Brent over the summer talking football, I heard about struggles that every program talks about. The battles were the same at Mankato West when I was the head coach, and at my two most recent high school assistant coaching stints in Prior Lake and Minnetonka. "Some kids are not committed." "Are we fast enough to win at a high level." "We are thin on the depth chart, and we have to stay healthy." "Some kids are using alcohol or drugs; we need to address it." "So and so has a bad attitude, how do we address it?" These are among the challenges high school football is facing.

The answers to these questions and doubts are simple. They have to be addressed with honesty and direct communication. All adversity must be confronted. It's simple, but not easy. And because we live in an "easy, comfortable" society, often these issues are not appropriately addressed. In Caledonia, if you are a player that fits one of the above categories, you are going to talk with Carl Fruechte. It's going to be clear, direct, and honest, even if it ruffles some feathers.

Be Willing to Lose so You can Win.

When adversity or controversy arises, you have to be willing to lose so you can win. What does that mean? If an athlete is cancer to the team, he has to be addressed. If it continues? He has to be removed from the team or situation, even if he's your best player. Will you lose without him? Possibly. Will it hurt the team? Probably. But unless the case is faced head-on, it will tear the fabric of your culture apart. There's no question about it. When the team knows you are prepared to lose a game or two to succeed in the long run, they will rally around this posture. As a result, discipline issues will start to fade. Coach means business. There's absolutely no question the Caledonia staff means business. The players know this and act accordingly. Leave no doubt in this area. Demand character from yourself, your staff, and the team. The results will then begin to build in your favor. But remember, you have to hold people accountable. If accountability starts to slip, so will the results.

That's great for the athletes. So what about the parents? There's no doubt that parents today are often helicopters. When I played, in the mid-90s, parents did not call the coach about playing time. Parents didn't reach out if a player got his feelings hurt. Parents today are smothering their kids, not coaching them. It's undeniable, many parents are off their rockers, and they are hurting their kids. Podcast superstar and former Navy SEAL Jocko Willink offers invaluable parenting advice. "If you help your kids, you are hurting them." Does this mean you don't make them dinner and provide for their basic needs? No. That's not what he is saying. Does this mean you ignore them and make them do everything themselves? No, he doesn't propose that. In my opinion, what Jocko means is you teach your kids what they need to know: you help them; you train them; then, you let them figure it out.

How are kids going to learn to stand up for themselves? Kids need to be the ones talking to the coach, not the parents. Can you advise them? Yes, you can. It goes like this: "So Jimmy, you are upset about your playing time. You should go in and talk to the coach. I'm going to advise you what to say." You then advise little Jimmy on what to say, and he goes and talks to his coach, and he learns a formidable life lesson. What if Jimmy refuses? He learns that if you don't advocate for yourself, you may not advance in life. This is one example; a million-dollar lesson that will allow your kids to grow and learn. If you help them, you hurt them. As coaches, explain this to your parents and players. Set the expectation for the families in your program. It will help minimize the misery in your life.

What if a parent writes you a nasty email? Many coaches will take this personally, thinking that person hates them. Instead, see it as an opportunity. It's an inside look into what is going on in that athlete's world. That email can give you insight into how to coach that kid. A critical email also allows us to build character in the athlete. How? It's always my policy if you call or email me, I'm going to share all that information with your son promptly. Where did I learn this? Caledonia. Through observing Carl and his staff over the years. Honest, transparent, and direct communication is always the best way to handle adversity. I can attest to this method. Precise communication allows us to clear the air and speak truth— speak the truth, the honest, unvarnished truth. But do it in love. Don't be rude, but be firm. (Ephesians 4:15)

Questions:
Do you believe in yourself and the team? Do you think big and aim for perfection, even though you'll never reach perfection?

How do you handle adversity? Do you recognize adversity as an opportunity?

Do you have faith that if you continue to do the work, stay positive and think big good things will happen?

ATTRIBUTE #6

Work Harder on Yourself than Anyone Else. Character is King.

"But the Lord said to Samuel, "Do not look on his appearance or on the height of his stature, because I have rejected him. For the Lord sees not as man sees: man looks on the outward appearance, but the Lord looks on the heart." 1 Samuel 16:7 NIV

Success can make you a better person or expose your flaws. When success comes your way, you'll need to learn and grow. As leaders, if we fail to better ourselves when we experience success, we may lose the grasp we have on it. That's why consistent winning is so rare. When success finally comes, we must grow and learn to steward it, or else we lose it. If you don't improve as a leader with success, it can bring destruction. Reflect on how you respond to losing. If you don't manage it well, that's a sign that you won't handle consistent winning well either. You just won't be able to hide it. Winning reveals the cracks in our character as much or more than losing. If we are not on the path of constant self-improvement, winning will expose the arrogance and negative ego that every person struggles to control. The person you are should not change based on wins and losses, or success and failure. You need to prepare yourself for handling both winning and losing. When Coach Fruechte took over the Caledonia program in 1997, he was young and inexperienced. But the values he brought to the table have not changed. He's the same person now as he was back then. He's just more experienced.

How do I do that? How do I prepare myself to handle success and failure? To be brutally honest, most people don't know how to do this—I certainly didn't. I had to learn along the journey. As you mature, you hopefully start to figure it out. Start searching for knowledge and wisdom, so when opportunity for success arises, you are ready for it.

Work harder on yourself than you do anyone else. How does becoming a better person help the team? Wait, how does someone even work on becoming a better person?

As I walked into Mark Froehling's house to interview him, he had a stack of 5-6 books by his side on the table. They were worn down with sticky notes and note cards sticking out of them. It was apparent he didn't just read the books. He absorbed them. Walk into the coach's office at Caledonia High School or the basement at Carl Fruechte's house, and you'll see hundreds of books about faith, football, war, speed, and strength. How does this help teams win games? "If you want to be the best, you have to study the best. And not just read a book, you have to absorb it," said Carl. He reads all the time. Carl continued, "God demands we make ourselves better to serve him better. Fight against laziness and start doing things to improve yourself as a coach, teacher, and parent."

When Carl talks about absorbing leadership lessons, he means listening to great speakers and sermons. He suggests reading books and taking notes. I once loaned Carl my Zig Ziglar book. *See you at the Top*. I got it back, and he had forgotten he wrote all types of sticky notes in it. One said, "share this with Maria." Another note said, "this is great to share with the team," and so on. When you read good books and listen to positive, inspirational speakers instead of sports shows, television, and music, it rewires your brain. It is somewhat difficult to explain, but when a person reads books, they gain knowledge. They gain wisdom. There are stories in books that can be retold to the team. The information becomes RAM, or random access memory. You can pull stories out of your mind that can apply to situations and help the team learn. The things you learn can be drawn upon in times of struggle to inspire or to humble an undefeated team or even to rebuke behaviors. Read books, listen to great speakers, and podcasts. Take notes, highlight, and share the wisdom you gain with the team and coaches.

I remember using several stories to help get a particular point across to the team. My best example? I have several. How about the book by Jim Collins, *Good to Great*. The author asks Admiral Jim Stockdale about his experiences in the Hanoi Hilton, a prison camp in Vietnam. He specifically asks about who survived. Admiral Stockdale goes on to talk about who didn't make it. The optimists and the pessimists. The pessimists died in their negativity, and the optimists died because they always hoped they'd be out by a specific date. "We'll be out by Christmas." They were not out by Christmas. "We'll be out by Easter." They were not out by Easter. Hope failed, and they died. "You must never confuse faith that you will prevail in the end—which you can never afford to lose—with the discipline to confront the most brutal facts of your current reality, whatever they might be," shared Admiral Jim Stockdale. This is the story I read to our 2012 team at Mankato West. That year we had to forfeit four games because we unknowingly played an ineligible athlete. It helped get us through the season. The Admiral's account of what happened at the prison camp helped us keep faith. We won our section and advanced to the state playoffs. If I never read the book *Good to Great*, I wouldn't have this great story to share with our team. It may have helped us become section champions that year.

Working on yourself is possibly the number one concept people ignore. They will talk until they are blue in the face about X's and O's, scheme, or a specific part of the year-round program. All that stuff is essential, yes, but not as important as becoming a better version of yourself. Set goals to improve in every area of your life. Why? Because setting that goal and working to achieve it will be difficult, and doing difficult things makes us a better person. The process refines us and increases our ability to lead. Regardless of whether or not you actually reach the goal, the actual pursuit of achieving it can make you a better person because of the work, discipline, and adversity you fight through to get to the finish line. These are good things. Not things to be avoided. Go to work on yourself. Challenge yourself to get better. It will make everything around you better. It's almost magic.

Here are a few suggestions to become a better you. Find a few people that are living a life you want to live. If they are still around and accessible, spend time with them, and ask questions. If possible, forge a friendship with them. Surround yourself with positive friends who will be honest with you in a respectful way. Eliminate associations with those who waste time, cuss, and drink too much. Find a few good books and read one a month, taking notes and highlighting the parts you think apply to your team or situation. Download books on audio, listen to podcasts or watch YouTube videos of people that inspire you. Spend time with people that are more successful than you, people who can enlighten your spiritual outlook or people who have large amounts of knowledge to be shared.

Another vital part of self-improvement is becoming a better spouse and parent. If what is happening within your four walls is not in order, and there is no unity, how are you going to lead others? The answer is—you won't. At least not as effectively as you could. You must invest in your marriage and your family, especially during the season. It's meaningful to set time aside for both wife and children. It might be every Saturday night from 5 to 9 p.m. Or Sunday mornings followed by lunch at home. Shut-off the phone, don't check email. Be disciplined in this. After all, you preach discipline to your team, right? Now apply it to your life. My wife and I have time set aside each week to spend together — the same with the kids. The time I get home from practice until the kids are in bed is the time I spend with them. I've learned this by being around great men my whole life, starting with Carl Fruechte and Mark Froehling.

I also encourage you to set a physical goal and get rid of a bad habit. Are you one of those coaches who chews tobacco? Quit. Once again, apply the discipline you preach and then share your story with the team of how you quit. I guarantee sharing about a struggle you overcame will draw the team closer to you. It will also teach them not to chew tobacco. Carl used to drink seven bottles of diet soda every single day. He gave it up; he overcame the addiction. It made him a better person.

He preaches all the time to the kids not to drink soda. So it made his story even better when he gave it up himself.

What about a physical challenge? Mine is jiu-jitsu. You can start at any age. There are guys I train with that are 70-years-old who beat me. A lot of guys start in their 40s and 50s. Just get started if jiu-jitsu interests you. What about losing 50 pounds? Set your mind to it and go for it. Start an exercise program or weight lifting program. Start walking with your wife. You'll spend quality time with her, and it will help you reach a physical goal. Share stories of real-life struggles with the team, within reason, of course. Talk about past mistakes and what you've learned from them. Kids will be drawn to you because of your honesty. They will trust you more, and your relationship will grow with these young men. You will also become a better person.

"With all things being equal, the team with the greatest character will win." Pete Carroll.

Character is king. There's no question. When you get a talented team filled with high-character kids, that team is unstoppable. But character starts with the head coach. If you lack character, so will the team. Hey, wait a minute. I am a high-character person, but my team doesn't reflect that. What's up with that? The answer to that question is simple. You may be a person who does it the right way, many coaches are, but you are not communicating and teaching that to the team. Yes, your team watches you and learns from what you do. Yes, they see you make good choices. But the theme of this book is high-character habits must be preached and taught all the time. It's a five-minute talk with the team before or after practice. It's a one-on-one conversation with a kid. It's when that group of players comes to your office during lunch. You use that time to instill the values you feel are essential. You talk about life and what's going on. You talk about the right way to treat a girlfriend. You talk about why cuss words are not productive and why we aren't going to allow them. You talk about why manners are so important in life. You teach, teach, and teach some more. Communicate the character that's inside you. It will come alive and attach itself to the team. Never assume that communication has been accomplished. That's why I use the word "preach" when I talk about Caledonia football. The coaches are preachers. Carl, Brent, Ernie, and the rest of the staff are always talking about character issues with the players. When Carl raises his voice before a game and says, "I don't want boys, I want you to be men." The kids understand what he's saying because the groundwork has been laid.

Character development is similar to your running game. You decide what 4-5 run concepts you want to teach for the season. Then you spend the entire season attempting to perfect those schemes. It's like running a defense. You have your top secondary coverages that you run each year, and you try to improve those coverages with hundreds or thousands of reps. You spend a lot of time on the scheme and techniques. Then, you see improvement each week in running the ball or running the coverages. It's no different when it comes to character development. Decide what your program stands for. What are the top 10 characteristics you want your team to be about? Practice them, teach them, tell stories about yourself, and others to drive the point home. Tell stories you read in books or hear on podcasts to drive the point home. Rep character every day. You won't be perfect at it, just like your run game is never perfect. But you can get really darn good at it if you give it reps. What you pay attention to will increase. Focus on character.

Talent wins games. Talent makes the sale. Talent is a prince. Character is the king. Character is a combination of our entire being. It's an intangible that can't be measured. When kids start to find value in being around the program because you are teaching life skills that work, you are going to find that more and more kids want to be around you. The program will start to thrive. Kids who leave the program after graduation will want to come back to see you. They will want to talk to you about life and seek your wisdom. They will want to help out as volunteer coaches. You will build an incredible alumni base, but also lifelong friendships with former players.

Let's learn from Coach Fruechte. Carl is continually using football as a teaching tool for life. He is consistently drawing analogies from struggles faced in high school and on the football field that will help young men when they become a husband and father. The difficulties of training for football, the discipline of working out and training year-round, getting up early, staying late, and playing a tough game, Carl is always making connections between football and life because he genuinely wants his players to be better people. Building better, tougher men in the community that are great husbands and great fathers—remember that's Carl's purpose.

Josh Gran, Zach's younger brother, sums it up in his own words. "Going through the Caledonia football program is more valuable than any education you are going to get. You'll never understand what it means until you've been through it. You have to experience it to understand why we are the way we are." Josh gives credit for his success in life to being part of this extraordinary program. He recently gave a presentation for a promotion at his workplace. "My whole presentation revolved around Caledonia football. Who I am and why I've had success at work to this point. It's all about what I learned from Caledonia football," Josh acknowledged.

Questions:

What are you doing to become a better person? What books can you read, what podcasts can you listen to?

Why is character important to you? Write this down and share this with your team.

How can you instill character into the people you lead?

ATTRIBUTE #7

Create the Brotherhood.

A friend loves at all times, and a brother is born for a time of adversity. Proverbs 17:17 NIV

Coach Fruechte believes that hard work, discipline, and having fun with your teammates creates a brotherhood. This includes: getting up early to get to the weight room, going through the difficult work out with your teammates, or in Caledonia's case, with your brothers; attending team camp in the summer; driving to 7-on-7 tournaments and speed camps. It also involves spending time together, working hard, going through adversity, and finally being taught that you can have fun and be serious at the same time. Learning that you are doing this to benefit the greater good of the teammate next to you. The attitude Coach Froehling aimed for when he took over the program has become a reality under Carl's leadership. Kids are now playing hard and trying their best, not just to hit someone hard, but to do their job for the brother next to them. Being part of a team is committing to doing your job well, and trusting the person next to you will also do theirs.

Don't mess with the brotherhood either. When kids feel unity, the sense of a real team, they become unstoppable if you try to hurt or mess with one of their own. Former middle linebacker Zach Kasten remembers when one of his buddies, Colin Coughfield, was kicked in the ribs. It was a dirty play. Carl Fruechte saw it and went off, yelling at the officials from the sideline. Colin came back to the huddle in obvious pain and very unhappy. The Warrior huddle was livid. The opponent just kicked one of their brothers. "That just amplified our intensity. It was on after that point," Zach said. The Warriors amped up their game. But they weren't about to do it illegally. If a Warrior kicked or punched another player, the yellow flag would be nothing compared to facing

Carl on the sideline. Unethical play is not tolerated. If a kid played dirty, he'd be pulled and talked to— loudly. I recently attended a playoff game in Caledonia. One player was absent from the lineup. Where was he? Suspended for punching an opposing player in a previous game. The punches didn't even draw a flag from the officials. They just didn't see it. But it was brought to Carl's attention, and a suspension followed.

The Warriors get revenge, but with clean play. "A lot of teams think we are a dirty team. Coach would have no part of that," recalled Zach Kasten. "We'd always just go after kids at a higher level; we got more fired up when teams played dirty. You paid back until the whistle blew, you did it the right way. Nothing cheap, no words." That's the Caledonia way. There is a calmness in their play. Zach's comments were edified at the playoff game I attended. Caledonia was up big in the third quarter. After a kickoff, one of the opposing players laid a cheap shot on a Caledonia player, then shoved the kid's head into the ground and started talking smack. The whole bench told the Caledonia player to get up and shouted praise to him as he walked away. "Way to go! Let them play dirty! Walk away!" The brotherhood holds each player accountable.

This football family not only holds the players responsible but also helps police the team. Great teams will police themselves. This "self-policing" comes from years of character development and players knowing team expectations. Zach Kasten recalled another story; "We had one kid that transferred to Caledonia and was doing some dirty stuff on the field. I told Coach Schroeder to pull him and not let him play the rest of the game. I told Coach just to trust me, and he did. We watched the film later on and saw the dirty plays. He was happy he pulled that player," Zach said.

How did the brotherhood begin? Many schools try to achieve the caliber of the Warriors' football program, but the feeling of being brothers wasn't always prevalent in Caledonia. As we found out in the '80s and '90s, it was absent. What was the spark that got this entire thing moving in the right direction? First, the coaching staff is always teaching and training, talking about brotherhood, sharing stories, and sharing examples. That's how it first got started. Then there's a key transition by putting the philosophies into action. In Caledonia, there is sacrifice and service among the more seasoned players who work with younger players. And then, of course, the hard work that comes with being a football player.

Brotherhood is formed when a team sweats together, bleeds together, and faces adversity together, and these experiences must be accompanied by proper teaching from the leadership. Then came the initial success. The Caledonia coaches captured and capitalized upon that success by humbling themselves and seeking wisdom. Remember, it was Carl who reached out to Dale Baskett to learn more about speed *after* the first state title. The humility of the coaching staff and their accountability to the Warrior brotherhood keep the team from getting a "big head." Personal growth of the staff, led by Carl, of course, allows the team to hold on to consistent success. But remember, success doesn't always translate to winning a state title. It is when kids start to "get it"—that is the sweet spot of Caledonia's success. I hear a lot of coaches say, "that kid doesn't get it." For the most part, they are probably correct in saying that. Keep in mind; it's your job to teach it. If they don't "get it" then you have to explain it. Then your team can hit their sweet spot.

"The brotherhood started because we played together before seventh grade. The youth environment was awesome, the older guys always welcomed us. Even if we had our differences, we always had each other's back," recalled Zach Kasten. "I grew up watching Karl and Kevin Klug, and then the state championship teams in '07 and '08. It was just always something I wanted to be a part of. The varsity kids would run the youth practices, and we loved it. Those guys were heroes to us," he said.

"This is a brotherhood, there is no doubt about it," Kasten confidently stated. "You can't do it yourself" is the motto of the coaching staff. The trash talk from the other team always seemed to increase with the score. "Did you hear what that kid said?" "Yeah, it's time to get after it." The level of play increased. The opponent paid the price. Maybe someday you'll catch Caledonia when they are an average team, and you'll get away with it. But during this twenty-three year stretch? Just don't talk smack. Save yourself the headache.

After all the stories we hear about Coach Fruechte and Caledonia, does this team have any fun? The intensity and passion that the staff brings to the game. The brutal honesty when you make a mistake. The occasional butt-chewing. Getting up every morning to lift and run speed workouts. How can all this be fun?

One Man's Sport is Another Man's Hell.

Fun is relative. What one person thinks is fun, another person might think is nonsense. What's fun about the Caledonia football culture? Pretty much everything. Once a person learns that setting and achieving goals is fulfilling, it becomes fun. Even if the "fun" is hell for another person, in fact, the more difficult the goal, the more enjoyable working to achieve it can be. Kids realize that fun is being held accountable and maintaining discipline. Yes, it's ok to cut loose and relax. But striving and working toward a strenuous goal is rewarding. It's fun to have Carl Fruechte, the no-nonsense leader, cut loose and crack a joke. It's fun to travel with him and get to know him as he plays the drums on the steering wheel of the school van and sings terribly off-key to the '80s music on the radio. It's fun to be around Ernie Hodges and Brent Schroeder. To get to know them and find out they are real human beings with struggles just like anyone else.

For the players, it's the brotherhood, banding together to accomplish a goal that only a team can achieve. That's fun. You can't do it by yourself. Being part of a team that is on the same page, loves each other, and is experiencing high-level success. That's fun. But most of all, it's extraordinarily fun to be involved in something bigger than yourself. Greg Hoscheit sums it up perfectly. "It's like a wheel, each spoke in the wheel plays a role and supports the other spokes," Hoscheit said. That's why so many people want to be involved. Whether it's a member of the booster club, loyal fans, players, coaches, or volunteers, all are spokes that lead to the wheel being fully supported. That's fun, especially when it's paired with winning. For Caledonia, the spokes had to be put in place before the consistent winning took place. So do the work and have fun. Believe that victory will come. But remember, winning does not equal success. When winning shows up, be ready to capture it and humbly build on it.

Questions:
What can you do to develop brotherhood in your team?

Does your team bond through hard work, or do they just do the work to get by?

How can you create a bond through team activities and hard work?

ATTRIBUTE #8

Use This Stuff in Life.

Nathan Bahr had dreams of becoming a doctor. He graduated from Caledonia High School in 2001 then went to Loras College in Iowa for his undergraduate degree. From there, Nathan moved on to medical school at Loyola University in Chicago. He then went on to his internal medicine residency at the University of Minnesota, Twin Cities. His next step at the U of M was an infectious disease fellowship. Nathan is now an infectious disease doctor that spends a good portion of his time traveling to Uganda, where he helps the downtrodden and less fortunate fight communicable diseases.

As Nathan reflects on his days at Caledonia High School, where he was a talented lineman, he can't help but think of the lessons he took away from the program—lessons he has used in life. "First of all, I remember learning humility from Carl." Nathan laughed as he recalled one specific moment during his senior year. The Warriors were at a scrimmage, and the line play was struggling, Nathan was frustrated and so was Carl. The offensive line huddled together as Carl helped them break down some of the problems they were having.

"Nathan, are you getting your job done?" Carl asked. Nathan responded in a slightly abrupt tone, "Of course I'm getting my job done." Carl's response is something Nathan will remember forever. Carl grabbed his shoulder pads and looked directly into Nathan's eyes. "I don't care if you are a senior and our best lineman if you continue to talk like that you won't play!" Nathan noted the seriousness in Carl's demeanor. To this day, he understands that it's essential to be a humble part of the team. Everyone is replaceable. Nathan believes humility will lead to being a good teammate. Being a humble member of a team is a life skill. Linemen rarely get credit in football. He learned to accept his role humbly, and it's a big reason he can work well with a team of over 50 doctors, nurses, and lab technicians as they travel to Africa. "Carl always told us to be humble and stressed the team first," said Nathan.

Carl is one of the few mentors in life that Bahr tries to connect with consistently. They'd often connect in Minneapolis when Carl came up to watch Isaac's games. Or, they'd grab lunch when he was back in Caledonia. "I took a lot away from my time at Caledonia and my time with Carl." Nathan doesn't pursue fame or fortune. He wants to help the less fortunate. That's why Nathan travels to Africa. He uses his skills in life, and Carl is proud of him.

Applying these Skills in my Life.

My wife Sarah and I stared at each other in disbelief. Knots turned in our stomach as we listened to what was about to unfold. For the past 17 years, we enjoyed working side-by-side running our home based business. We struggled and fought our way from nothing and grew it into something that fulfilled us and provided a significant income for our family. However, we were about to learn we'd lose most of what we had worked for. Our buddy Brad called to tell us about a big announcement happening the next day. The company was going to make changes to its compensation plan. We would lose 98 percent of our income. Sarah and I dialed up trusted friends—both in life and business—Joe and Gloria. "Is this true? Is it really happening?" They confirmed the news. It was a bombshell.

I'd like to tell you I just shrugged this off and said we'd be fine, but that would be a lie. Panic set in. The next week was filled with agony. We eventually found out the company was hit with a frivolous set of charges. However, it seemed as though this company was unwilling to fight for the people who had invested so much time and effort to grow the customer base. We felt betrayed, almost like we were cheated by a good friend and taken for everything we had.

The experience has been surreal. There are many unknowns as the story continues to unfold. Carl Fruechte and Ernie Hodges were two of the first people I talked to after hearing the news. They were both ears that listened to my plight. Their response helped me refocus. "You'll be fine; things will work out. God has a plan." Yes, God does have a plan. My wife and I put our faith in Him. We continued to pray for direction and provision for our family. He provided. With some help from our good friend Bill Marks in Mankato, Minnesota, I was able to take a part-time teaching and assistant coaching job in Minnetonka, Minnesota under legendary football coach Dave Nelson. A handful of part-time job opportunities in the fitness industry opened up for Sarah. People came through for us and volunteered to help. Our friends offered to serve us in any way. What was the end result? I wish I could tell you, as I write this book, the story is in progress.

All I know is that we will fight. I learned how to fight the battle in front of me when I was at Caledonia. We will never quit. We will work hard and remain humble. We will still dream big and set goals. We found out in a real way, inside adversity lies opportunity. People will look at you when things fall apart and watch how you react. How did we respond? We took the high road, surrounded ourselves with positive thinkers, and saturated ourselves in God's promises. We know in the end everything will work out. When Carl checked in on me with a text a week or so after the news hit, my response was, "Carl, I'm a Brownsville boy, I'll figure this out." Carl responded, "I know you will!" Brownsville boys know how to fight. Fortunately for me, it's not physical. It's a mental and emotional fight, and Sarah and I have taught our family how to do battle as well. I know Carl is proud of that.

This Program is Changing People.

I stood in a parking ramp outside U.S. Bank Stadium, waiting to pay my parking fees. The Caledonia Warriors did it again! They beat Minneapolis North 26-0 to clinch another state title—

Making it five in a row, and a 68-game winning streak. There was a small line ahead of me waiting to pay for parking, as well. It was a group of 5-6 people wearing Caledonia attire, ranging in age from about 50 to 80-years-old. "Caledonia football sure is amazing," said one person in the line. Everyone agreed. "They are amazing, they got a hold of my grandson, Sam," one woman said, "they changed him. He turned into such a polite young man. He still is." Then another responded, "Yes, the program teaches more than football. They teach these kids about life." Hearing these comments, I thought about all the untold stories of Caledonia football. How many stories are out there that need to be told? It's impossible to fit them all into one book. I reflected on my time at Caledonia High School...how many boys that were my age and older would have had a different trajectory of life with a program in place like it is now?

The current Caledonia staff has taught life proficiency since the beginning. But as Carl matured, he has improved his teaching ability— he has become wiser. "This is going to prepare you for life," is something you often hear Caledonia coaches tell the kids. Carl Fruechte has consistently stated such things as:

"You don't get second chances in life."
"Things are going to get tough in life, with your wife, raising kids".
"You can't quit in football, and you can't quit in life. If you do, there are consequences. Whether you intend for it or not, there are consequences."

"Showing up for morning speed workouts is just like showing up to a job every morning."
Giving everything in the weight room and the football field can lead to someone giving their all in life."

This is true as long as it's taught to the kids, provided it comes with lessons, with stories and examples that drive the point home. You can't just tell the kids, you have to teach the kids. That's what Carl is great at.

Consistent role modeling and sharing lessons are vital practices that can trigger culture change. Kids respond because they know what they are being taught is true. The players see men in the community living out what the Caledonia football staff is preaching. And it starts with the man in charge, but also encompasses the men on staff and in the community. There's a multiplier, the more men that come out of the program and return to Caledonia, the more common it is to be uncommon. If the current staff continues to coach for 20 more years, the town will be full of champions in life.

One top-notch man that models this life is Brad King, a member of the Caledonia football staff and head basketball coach. Brad married Carl's sister, Susan Fruechte, and settled down in the city where he grew up. Brad and Susan started a family and have worked hard to provide for that family. They have four great kids: first came their daughter Alexis, then the three boys; Owen, Noah, and Eli—all talented athletes.

I always looked up to Brad and Susan, even though I didn't know them well. While in school, I observed how they carried themselves on the basketball court and was impressed. They are exceptional examples in the Caledonia community. Coincidentally, they are also great parents. How do I know they're great parents? Watch their kids. How does this relate to Caledonia football? Their two oldest sons happen to be undefeated as starting quarterbacks over the last five years. But there's more to it than that. It's the way Owen, Noah, and Eli have carried themselves on and off the field. Through unbelievable stress, these boys stay calm and focused, cool, and collected. It's the epitome of what is preached in the Caledonia program, and at home.

"We always taught the kids to treat people the way they'd want to be treated," Brad King said. He continued, "We taught the boys if someone is being mistreated, they need to step up and say or do something." Combine the skills the King's teach at home with what's taught in the Caledonia football program and it will undoubtedly produce champions.

Before the football program changed the school culture, it was easy for good kids to get swept up in the negativity— or quite simply just go unnoticed. The culture change that has occurred in the program allows for positive life skills to emerge in an entire community.

The Greatness in Caledonia Football

When I entered the weight room at Caledonia High School a few weeks ago, I noticed an article taped by the door that said something like, "Why teenagers don't need a smartphone." I didn't stop to read it. I knew why it was there. The Caledonia coaches think most kids are addicted to phones and computers. In fact, after I watched Caledonia roll over St. Charles for their 64th win in a row, Carl huddled the guys up and told them they had a little time off. "Don't waste your downtime by sitting in front of a computer," Carl advised. It's excellent advice. In fact, it's so simple the kids don't truly realize they are learning a life skill.

Embedded in everything Caledonia has done, there is a recurring theme—use the stuff you learn through the great game of football to make your life better. Kids across the country have learned many life skills by playing athletics. Carl and the Caledonia coaches have intentionally drawn the parallel from football to life. In a recent press conference following a win in the state semi-final game, Carl was quoted as saying, "God first, family second, school third and athletics fourth." The quote sums up how Carl orders his life. I can't think of a better way to prioritize. Most people in our country are never taught how to prioritize their lives. They just drift through life, not knowing what they value.

The appeal of Carl is he is down to earth. He's not average, but he lives average. He lives with humility the way Christ did. Former players still want to make him proud, and they know they can do that by living a good life. They don't have to be rich and famous—be humble, work hard, give back, and be willing to sacrifice. That's what makes Carl proud. Start with just your own life. Figure out what you want to do and seek your purpose. Get married and provide for your wife and children, not only financially, but by investing in them. Build the best marriage and raise great kids. Then take a deep breath and look around; you've provided for your wife and kids, now who else can you invest in? Have faith, give back, and dream big. Your biggest dream might not lead you out of Caledonia, and that's ok. Carl's vision for you is that you'll give your best and strive to be your best. Aim for perfection, you will never reach the pinnacle, but going all out will make you uncommon. But above all, more important than anything you could possibly achieve, is your relationship with God. If you only do one thing, and one thing only—put your faith and trust in Jesus Christ. That's Carl Fruechte, and that's Caledonia.

How some of the players mentioned in this book are succeeding in life:

Karl Klug played eight seasons with the Tennessee Titans. Coach Fruechte was the first person Karl called when his football career ended. He now uses the lessons he has learned in football to raise his family. Karl and his wife have four children. He also coaches high school football.

Kevin Klug played football at Minnesota State University, Mankato. He graduated from the Division II school then moved to Nashville, near his brother. Kevin runs a successful business called *Klug Fitness*.

John Hauser, Carl's first quarterback, went on to be successful in business with his wife, Amy. He has earned the time freedom to help coach football. John currently coaches the quarterbacks at Caledonia. He has helped produce some outstanding leaders.

Jesse Nelson continues to serve our country as a U.S. Navy SEAL.

Zach Gran got out of the Navy SEALs and is a mortgage banker in Cedar Falls, Iowa.

Ryan Pitts passed on an opportunity to play college athletics and decided to go to a technical college. He recently became engaged to Alexis King. Ryan started his own business, Vision Media LLC, and coaches football and track for Caledonia.

Troy Frank is the working supervisor at Lock and Dam #8 on the Mississippi River. He married Carl's oldest daughter Alecia. Troy is raising his son, loving his wife, and experiencing true success in life.

Zach Hauser is a Physical Education teacher at Caledonia High School and the head football coach at Spring Grove High School. He has led his team to two state championships.

Kody Moore helps out at a dairy farm and helps Zach Hauser win state championships at Spring Grove.

Eddie Hodges followed in the footsteps of his dad Ernie. He loves strength and conditioning. Eddie trains professional football players and runs his own fitness business. He also helps out in Caledonia with the football program.

Josh Gran was just promoted in the finance department of a large business. He also served one term as mayor of Caledonia. Josh was 21 when he was elected—the youngest mayor in the town's history.

Zach Kasten is a farmer. He's married and recently had his first child. His two brothers also played football at Caledonia High School. His dad was a part of the 1976 state championship team. All four of them have won state championships.

Derek Adamson has worked at Wiebke Fur for the last 20 years. He is married with three children.

Nathan Bahr works at the University of Kansas and travels to Uganda as an infectious disease doctor.

Carl, Brent, and Ernie continue to write the Caledonia legacy.

Follow Rise of the Warriors on Facebook or on Twitter at @ROTW2019

ABOUT THE AUTHOR

Mark Esch is a 1995 graduate of Caledonia High School. He received his Bachelor of Science degree in Health and Physical Education with a coaching emphasis from the University of Wisconsin-La Crosse. Mark received his Master's degree from the University of South Dakota in Exercise Science. He has coached football for 18 years including 11 seasons as a head coach at Mankato West High School in Mankato, Minnesota. Mark, his wife and three daughters live in Savage, Minnesota.

Made in the USA
Columbia, SC
30 December 2019